A THOUSAND MIRACLES

THEODOR MERON, CMG

A Thousand Miracles

From Surviving the Holocaust to Judging Genocide

HURST & COMPANY, LONDON

First published in the United Kingdom in 2026 by
C. Hurst & Co. (Publishers) Ltd.,
New Wing, Somerset House, Strand,
London, WC2R 1LA

© Theodor Meron, 2026

All rights reserved.

Printed in Scotland by Bell & Bain Ltd, Glasgow

Distributed in the United States, Canada and Latin America by Oxford University Press, 546 Fifth Avenue, New York, NY 10036, United States of America.

The right of Theodor Meron to be identified as the author of this publication is asserted by him in accordance with the Copyright, Designs and Patents Act, 1988.

A Cataloguing-in-Publication data record for this book is available from the British Library.

ISBN: 9781805265238

EU GPSR Authorised Representative
Easy Access System Europe Oü, 16879218
Address: Mustamäe tee 50, 10621, Tallinn, Estonia
Contact Details: gpsr.requests@easproject.com, +358 40 500 3575

www.hurstpublishers.com

The author, then aged five, with his
older brother (left).

In memory of Monique Jonquet-Meron (1934–2023)
My love, my compass, my greatest miracle

CONTENTS

Preface xi

1. Surviving the Second World War 1
2. Farewell to Europe 21
3. In the Promised Land and Beyond 29
4. In Israel's Diplomatic Service 43
5. Against the Settlements in the Occupied West Bank: My Palestine Opinions 55
6. Becoming a Scholar 75
7. Poland and I 93
8. At the Rome Conference: The Birth of the International Criminal Court 101
9. In the US State Department: The Ups and Downs of a Judicial Nomination 109
10. From the Chair to the Bench 121
11. Life at The Hague 131

12.	The State of International Criminal Justice	155
13.	Commemorating Srebrenica and Reflecting on Genocide	173
14.	Surviving the Acquittal of General Gotovina	179
15.	Oxford Redux	187
16.	From the Bench to the Bar: Prosecuting Ukraine and Gaza War Crimes	197
17.	Please Do Not Leave Me	209

Appendix 217

PREFACE

Monique was not in favour of my writing a memoir. She felt that my OUP book *Standing up for Justice* (2021) was enough. Had she been alive, I would not have written it but her sudden death made me wish to write a book which would be a legacy to her.

I am grateful to Trinity College, Oxford, its President, Dame Hilary Boulding, and my colleagues at Trinity for their support and encouragement. And my deep gratitude to my friend Isabelle Lambert for her advice and help. Many thanks to Professors Stephen Fisher and Wolfgang Ernst for their suggestions.

Particular thanks to Zoe Flood for her vital support throughout this project and for recommending Hurst as publisher and suggesting the title (*A Thousand Miracles*, inspired by Jesse Eisenberg's film *A Real Pain*).

I am grateful to Michael Dwyer, publisher and managing director of Hurst Publishers for his interest and support, as well as that of his very professional team, and my editor Russell Martin for his excellent editing.

I thank my sons Daniel and Amos for their support and understanding.

1

SURVIVING THE SECOND WORLD WAR

It is 27 January 2020, the seventy-fifth anniversary of the liberation of Auschwitz by the Red Army, and the annual United Nations (UN) day of commemoration of the victims of the Holocaust, which resulted in the murder of one-third of the Jewish people, millions of Poles and Russians, and countless Roma. I am in the UN General Assembly hall where in a little while I am to deliver the keynote speech at the invitation of Antonio Guterres, the UN Secretary-General.

So many memories from the past flood my mind – from this hall, first and foremost. I first came here in 1961 as a young member of the Israeli Permanent Mission to the United Nations and stayed till 1966. I returned in 1975 as a Rockefeller Foundation fellow to do a book on the UN Secretariat. And, of course, after 2003, as president of the International Criminal Tribunal for the former Yugoslavia, a UN war crimes tribunal, I had to be here once a year to speak from this very same podium.

Other memories come streaming in, though I try not to let them overwhelm me: memories of the Holocaust, which for so long I tried to forget or, at least, to control, and never, or almost

A THOUSAND MIRACLES

never, to speak about. To these is added my usual fear of public speaking, which I learned to tame or hide over the years. I worry that my voice will break down, that my emotions will take over.

I am called for a photographic session with the dignitaries and guests who will speak. These include the UN Secretary-General, whom I like and respect, the ambassadors of Germany, Israel, Russia and the United States, two survivors of the Holocaust who came from Israel for this event, a representative of the Roma, and Itzhak Perlman, who will come later to make a brief musical contribution.

The General Assembly hall is full of people. Among them are my wife Monique, my sons Dan and Amos and their children, my former wife, Roxandra, UN delegates, and friends. Carolyn Willson is also in the hall. She is an ex-US diplomat and a friend who was with me in Rome in 1998 for the conference to establish the International Criminal Court. She was my election officer from the US Mission to the United Nations when in 2001 I campaigned for my first election by the General Assembly as a judge. Also present is Jean Galbraith, my brilliant law clerk at The Hague in 2007–8 and now a Penn Law School professor, who has long been a friend. Here too is the assistant secretary-general and deputy legal counsel, Stephen Mathias, a friend from my days in the US State Department in 2000–1, as well as many others.

All of this only adds to the pressure. So does the fact that I am to speak towards the end of the programme. In some ways, it is the most personal, most difficult and perhaps most important speech I will ever make. I try to keep my mind focused on listening to the speeches that are being delivered. One of the two Holocaust survivors, Mrs Irene Shashar, is now speaking. Her main point appears to be that Hitler did not win. He did not win because, despite his best efforts, she survived, she is here today, addressing this audience. Did he really not win? At least in part?

SURVIVING THE SECOND WORLD WAR

To kill one-third of a people, by far most of those within the geographical reach of his evil troops, and destroy forever whole communities, traditions and cultures was, alas, not a failure.

She and her fellow speaker talk about being Holocaust survivors. But in my speech I want to speak about the universal implications of the Holocaust and the importance of not letting atrocities happen, not being a bystander. I think of Martin Luther King's admonition that an individual has not started living until they can rise above the narrow confines of their personality and embrace the broader concerns of all humanity.

My turn now comes. Under-secretary-general Melissa Fleming introduces me briefly. In my speech, I try to make clear that the German killing machine did not target Jews only but also Roma, Poles, Russians and others, and I acknowledge those – the Just – who risked their lives to save Jews:

> It is often forgotten that millions of Poles and Russians also fell victim to the Nazi killing machine. I grieve for them all.
>
> The events of the Holocaust may seem far away to many of you, separated as they are from us by decades of progress. But for those who lived through them, as I did as a boy in occupied Poland, they are all too real. When I was nine, Nazi Germany invaded, I was overnight a refugee, out of school, out of childhood, and constantly in clear and present danger.
>
> What followed was the ghettos, work camps, and most of my family falling victim to the Holocaust.
>
> Even during those apocalyptic times, with so many Poles hostile and antisemitic, there were moments of light, with some Polish Catholics risking their lives to save Jews, some in my own family. In the dark sea of antisemitism and collaboration that swept occupied Europe, there were some islands of light. The saving of its entire Jewish population by the people of Denmark will remain forever as a rare epitome of true humanism.

A THOUSAND MIRACLES

I find it striking that a country that was as antisemitic as Poland produced per capita the highest number of righteous gentiles, non-Jews who saved Jews, recognized as such by Yad Vashem in Israel.

And, yes, there are stories of bravery and righteousness, of individuals standing up to be counted when the time to do so has come. I think of the young German soldier who found my maternal grandparents in their hiding place and, risking his life, decided not to turn them in. They thus survived for a few more months until caught in the Nazi net.

I think of the Warsaw Catholic baker who sheltered a little girl for all those years, risking her life and that of her own daughter.

I think of Aristides de Sousa Mendes, the Portuguese consul in Bordeaux who in defiance of orders saved thousands of Jews by giving them visas and who was, as a result, destroyed by Salazar, or the Pole Jan Karski who infiltrated the Warsaw Ghetto and an extermination camp and then travelled to the west to report to the Allies on the unbelievable destruction that was being inflicted on the Jews. Alas, bombing rail lines to the death camps was not on the Allies' priority list.

It is from acts of humanity that seeds of reconciliation and a shared sense of humanity emerge. Remembrance and acknowledgement of historic crimes, coming clean with the past, is essential to the process of reconciliation.

I pay homage to President Chirac, who, breaking with a long taboo, accepted the responsibility of France for Vichy's collaboration in the enforcement of the Holocaust, for committing, in his words, "the irreparable".

I speak of what is still to me a mystery of the Holocaust:

The shattering acts of the Holocaust still defy logic and belief. Of course, mass atrocities, even genocides, have been committed throughout history. But the Holocaust was the first industrial genocide. That hatred, bigotry, and antisemitism could lead to an amazingly

SURVIVING THE SECOND WORLD WAR

efficient technological, scientifically informed, bureaucratically run death machine and to continent-wide losses, not only of individuals, families, and whole communities but of basic humanity and shared human dignity as well, boggles the mind even now. They were of a sort that the world has never seen.

That people as cultured and educated as Germans could accept being ruled by monsters such as Hitler, a personification of absolute evil, and that peoples of occupied Europe could largely collaborate with the enforcement of the Holocaust, remains a mystery and a stain. And if it could happen in the country of Bach, Goethe, and Kant, could it not, given the right circumstances, happen in any country?

Could the Holocaust have happened without those who diverted their eyes, closed their hearts and doors, the bystanders, not to mention the collaborators, those that denounced, delivered, and plundered? And could not most of us become perpetrators of genocide? That is why we must remain vigilant and make sure that genocides are never, anywhere, allowed to happen again.

I end the speech with the prayer that "neither we nor our children will be victims or, even worse, perpetrators of genocide" and, to paraphrase Sir Michael Howard's Holocaust speech before the Oxford Chabad Society, that we will not be "those who simply let this happen: thinking the kind of things, tolerating the kind of behaviour that ultimately makes genocides possible".[1]

The day after my speech I give a short interview to UNTV on the prevention of genocide:

> Even today, we see so many examples of ongoing, very brutal ethnic and religious slaughters. Some of these are actually, in legal terms, genocide. Today we are moving into a situation of rampant radical nationalism.
>
> It is against immigrants. It is against Muslims. It is against Jews.

---

[1] To view my speech, https://news.un.org/en/story/2020/01/1056122

A THOUSAND MIRACLES

We must beware of demagogues who preach religious, ethnic hatred. By being vigilant, we may prevent a repeat of what happened in the thirties and forties in Europe.

The Holocaust was a prime example of genocide. If we do not remember, if we do not learn the lesson of the Holocaust, we might let those situations be repeated.

I believe that for somebody with my background, to become a Judge to judge war crimes, genocides, and crimes against humanity, and to preside over such trials, is one of the wonders of my life.

We gave to those who were accused of genocide, crimes against humanity, and war crimes fair and decent trials. It is important to call the crimes by their name. Words have resonance. The definition of crimes has resonance. Judgments and credible judgments of international courts have resonance. By focusing on history, by focusing on understanding the Holocaust, we build a better future in which holocausts become less likely.[2]

∞

The invasion of Poland on 1 September 1939 by Nazi Germany brought an apocalyptic change in my life: from sweet, uneventful, pampered childhood to the horrors of fleeing from monsters.

I was born in 1930 in a small town, Kalisz, in western Poland to a Jewish family, traditionally in the lumber trade. I had a happy but, alas, short childhood. Before the war we had a large apartment in the centre of town, in a building which belonged to the family. It was within walking distance of the big parks, of the river, which, unlike now, was frozen for several months a year, providing a great place for skating, and of my grandfather's lumberyard, an ideal place to play hide-and-seek. My grandfather

---

[2] "How We Can Prevent Tomorrow's Genocides: A Conversation with War Crimes Expert, Theodor Meron", https://videos.un.org/en/2020/02/04/how-we-can-prevent-tomorrows-genocides-a-conversation-with-war-crimes-expert-theodor-meron/

lived in a large house next to the lumberyard and expected us to join him for dinner on Saturdays and holidays. The food was good and plentiful, but he was rather formal and a bit of an authoritarian, looking more like a Polish nobleman than a Jewish patriarch; and we, the children, did not feel at ease with him, if not outright afraid. My father was quite different. He was always kind, gentle, good with the children, while my mother was shy and helpful. As time goes on, I remember her less and less.

The park offered ideal opportunities for biking. My brother, who was five years older than me, was, at least in my opinion, a biking ace. He could steer with his feet, stand on the saddle – miraculous feats. My admiration for his prowess was boundless. All I could achieve was biking with my hands off the handlebars. And my skating was mediocre, though enthusiastic.

My first two years of school were uneventful. Later I heard how antisemitic Polish children were, but honestly I did not sense any hostility while at school. Perhaps I was not mature enough to notice. I remember plenty of Chopin. Patriotism was the thing and Chopin's 'Polonaise Militaire' was a recurrent accompaniment on national holidays.

Spending the summers at resorts was not customary in middle-class Jewish families. Instead the thing to do was to rent a peasant house in a village. I remember one such summer in a village nestling in deep forests. As an ardent dog lover, I wanted to play with a big and wild stray dog, which did not appreciate my courtship. Nor was I smart enough to take heed of his growling, which warned me to leave him alone. Eventually, I showed even greater stupidity by trying to ride him. He promptly threw me off and took a deep bite of my leg. A big scar still shows the effects. The immediate concern of my parents was whether we should go to the nearest physician for a rabies shot. That would mean a long trip by horse-drawn cart. Since the locals assured us that the dog was healthy and only temperamental, it was decided to stay put and hope for the best. It turned out he wasn't rabid, for otherwise I wouldn't be here to tell this story. I was happy not to have ruined our vacation, but later felt that my parents took a lot for granted.

One summer the family rented a large forested estate which came with a mansion. I was impressed by the private railway siding to transport the logged wood. Then there was one last memorable summer on the Vistula, the principal river of Poland. The Vistula was wide, shallow, full of sand shoals and little islands. I will never forget the intense happiness I felt while kayaking slowly on the river and playing Robinson Crusoe on the islands.

∞

The mood at home slowly became darker. My parents spoke about the growing persecution of Jews in Germany. There was some talk about offering to take in Jewish refugee children from Germany. I was strongly in favour, as I wanted someone of my own age to play with. But my parents said they had enough worries already.

Then, one day, when I was nine, all hell broke loose. We heard of the German invasion of Poland on 1 September 1939, and since Kalisz was not far from the German border (it was occupied two days later), we packed some essentials preparatory to fleeing before German troops entered the town. I don't remember how, but my father managed to acquire a peasant's cart with a horse. I doubt if he had driven one before. We were joined by my uncle Marcus, an older brother of my father (they were five brothers and two sisters), his wife and two daughters. Together with a mass of panicking people we headed east, away from the invading Germans. We had to move slowly, as the roads, narrow and bumpy, were crowded. There was chaos everywhere. The civilians on the road were joined by units of the

Polish army, some army trucks but primarily cavalry, retreating east. I admired the officers on their horses, and their impressive uniforms and shining equipment. They pushed ahead, far faster than us, though they were often blocked by the crowds on the road. From time to time, German planes flew overhead, sometimes dropping bombs.

At night, we would pull up on the side of the road, spread some blankets and try to sleep. We bought food in the villages on the way. It was pretty expensive. Once, when German planes came particularly close, we took shelter in the ditches on the side of the road. When the bombing stopped, we went back to our cart only to discover that our horse had been killed. From then on we had to carry everything ourselves. As we had no rucksacks, we each took a suitcase and abandoned the rest of our belongings as well as the cart, and continued on foot.

Some of the bridges on our way had already been destroyed by German bombing. We had to cross rivers on improvised bridges, often jumping over trees or planks between rocks or islets. I found those crossings pretty scary. After many days of walking we found ourselves in eastern Poland, hoping that we would be safe there and that the Polish army would finally manage to block the Germans. Then we heard that the Soviet Union had invaded eastern Poland. Only later did we learn of the shameful Molotov–Ribbentrop Pact of 23 August 1939, which enabled Germany and the Soviet Union to occupy and partition Poland between them. Poor Poland was thus forced to endure its fourth partition.

Many of the refugees continued east nevertheless. These included my uncle Marcus and his family, who survived the war. As for my uncle Leon, my father's youngest brother, he was in the Warsaw Ghetto and was deported to Treblinka, yet he too survived. His exceptional story deserves to be told. As the Warsaw Ghetto was being liquidated and its population deported en masse to Treblinka, the inhabitants no longer had any doubts about what awaited them at the terminus of the railway line. When they were put on the train, Leon and a friend made sure to take with them tools to break out. As the train slowed down while climbing a hill towards Treblinka, they managed to break some planks in the cattle wagon, open a sufficiently large hole, and jump out. The SS guards opened fire, but as it was getting dark, they missed. Leon and his friend escaped into the forest and were separated. Leon eventually crossed a wooden bridge over a river. On the other side, he was stopped by a German soldier who was mounting a checkpoint. The soldier told Leon that he must deliver him to an army post. Leon, who spoke perfect German, begged for mercy. The soldier understood that, if turned in, Leon would be promptly executed. Amazingly and clearly risking his life, he agreed to let Leon go. He told Leon there was a railway station nearby and gave him a piece of bread and money to buy some peasant clothes and a ticket to Warsaw. After all kinds of adventures, Leon got to Warsaw and found the friend from whom he had been separated. This friend had with him some diamonds, which they used to pay a peasant in a village close to Warsaw to shelter them for the duration of the German occupation. Both survived.

Instead of going east like my uncle Marcus and his family, my parents decided to go south-west to Częstochowa, where my maternal grandparents lived. I don't know if we would have fared better had we gone east, given that the Nazi invasion of the Soviet Union followed soon afterwards. But to head for Częstochowa was clearly a calamitous choice. Truth be told, there were clearly no good choices.

In any event, much of our extended family had come together in Częstochowa by the end of September 1939. Częstochowa is a medium-sized city in southern Poland well known to every Polish child because of the ancient monastery of Jasna Góra. It houses the shrine of the Black Madonna, which legend says saved the monastery from Swedish invaders in the seventeenth century and turned that war into a Polish victory. It is an important place of pilgrimage. It was in Częstochowa that my parents, my brother and I moved into my grandparents' apartment. My maternal uncle Felix lived there already and we were joined by my paternal grandparents and some cousins. I was the youngest in the family. There were few children in the same building and, as schools were closed, I had no companions of my age to play with and talk to. There were not many books in the apartment which I could read. And people were too anxious to try to give me lessons. The typical subject of conversation at home was what the Germans might do to us next and how we could survive.

For my brother, I was too young to be of interest. He must have found company, as he was often out. He did not talk much about his activities. Later, I heard that he was involved in the Jewish resistance. So I was left to myself, and walking alone was my principal pastime.

One day, I ventured into the suburbs to the limestone quarries in which my grandfather was the manager. They had been inactive since the beginning of the war and I enjoyed climbing on the rocks, which for me seemed like formidable mountains. Soon thereafter the quarries were confiscated from their Jewish owners, my grandfather was fired, and a German civilian took over as manager. But as nothing seemed to change on the ground, I could continue going there for a while. The German manager was actually quite nice to my grandfather and to me. On one occasion he sent us a sack of coal; on another a sack of potatoes. Winters were extremely cold there, food was scarce, and so these gifts were very welcome.

On another occasion, I tried to get close to the Jasna Góra Monastery, which was not too far away, but I was accosted by a group of Polish youngsters who shouted antisemitic curses at me. I was afraid they would beat me up, so I ran back home.

A THOUSAND MIRACLES

I would also go to the railway bridge, which became a shelter for me where I could day-dream. Soon thereafter it became the border of the ghetto and out of bounds. But until the spring of 1941, I could go there and stare for hours at the steam locomotives pulling trains to distant and mysterious destinations. Day-dreaming was my only resource. It helped me escape the dreary reality of the ghetto.

In the same apartment block which my maternal grandparents occupied, there was a pretty blonde woman. Unbelievably, I still remember her name, Helen Tenenbaum. She lived there with her husband, whose name I do not remember. She was the mistress of Paul Degenhardt, the commander of the German police, the Schutzpolizei. I wondered how the husband must have felt about his wife having sex with Degenhardt. They were probably given extra food and promised to be spared from the worst. But they were not. When our neighbourhood was eventually marched to the selection place, only the Jewish policemen and their immediate families were spared, at least for a time. The Tenenbaums were not given a reprieve by Degenhardt. Hauptmann Degenhart was convicted many years later, in 1965, and was sentenced to life imprisonment but was released for health reasons seven years later.

It did not take long for the Germans to order all Jews to wear armbands with a star of David, but I was still below the age at which wearing an armband was obligatory. From the conversations at home I knew that the German authorities required the Jewish community to pay them from time to time large amounts of money. Jewish men also had to join the work brigades. Although food and coal were scarce, life during the first few months in Częstochowa was still not terrible.

Then things started going bad, and from bad to worse. In April 1941, the Germans established a Jewish quarter, called "the big ghetto". Jews living outside were ordered to move within its boundaries, while non-Jews living there had to move out. It was strictly prohibited that residents could leave the ghetto, thus putting an end to my solo peregrinations. Since our apartment lay within the ghetto, we were fortunate not to have to move.

Over time, Jews from many other Polish towns were ordered to move to Częstochowa. As a result the ghetto became even more congested, and the Jewish council assigned the newcomers to apartments already inhabited. We were lucky not to be forced to accept additional people into our apartment.

What I missed greatly in our terribly crowded apartment was some privacy, a corner to myself; but there was none. Everything, even very intimate activities, would take place in the sight of others. My maternal grandfather had great difficulties urinating. I still remember how embarrassed I was when a few times a day my uncle Felix would insert a catheter into my maternal grandfather's penis to help him urinate. I can only imagine how embarrassed my grandfather was.

In 1942, the atmosphere in the ghetto increasingly became doom-laden. Everybody talked about the rumours of mass executions of Jews. To try to protect the family, my uncle Felix joined the Jewish police established by the Jewish council on orders from the German authorities. They were given police-type hats, armbands and sticks. In the streets of the ghetto there were more and more German police and Ukrainian SS. It was all very scary. Felix built a hideout for his parents, my maternal grandparents, next to the bathroom for use during the expected "selections" and deportations. At that time, I found the actions of Felix in joining the Jewish police quite natural – they made total sense – as everything he did was intended to save his family. Yet today I am more aware that he was at the same time a minor actor in the Nazi system of enforcement. Still, I cannot bring myself to be harsh on him. And, of course, he saved my life.

A THOUSAND MIRACLES

Doomsday arrived quickly. On 21 September 1942 the ghetto was surrounded by German police and the Ukrainian SS. It was Yom Kippur, the Day of Atonement, when Jews are supposed to fast and are at their weakest. Apparently, it was the preferred day for German deportations of Jews. No one was allowed into the streets. The following day, Jews were forced out from their homes, street after street, and marched to a selection place, to be sorted into those few who might stay and the many intended for slaughter. The liquidation of the ghetto lasted a couple of weeks.

My paternal grandparents, like all old people, did not pass the selection test and were sent to Treblinka. My father, on the other hand, passed the selection process successfully and was moved to the small ghetto. As a young and strong person, my brother had a decent chance of surviving. We later heard that he attacked a German officer, possibly Degenhardt himself, during the selection, as he preferred being shot right away to being sent to Treblinka. No such luck. The Germans understood what motivated him and forced him into a train.

This was apparently not the end of his story. Much later we heard from a survivor in Israel that in Treblinka he was assigned to a work group and lived to join the rebellion which put an end to the camp. The survivors fled to the forests. We do not know if he was killed during the rebellion or managed to escape to the surrounding forests and was killed there by the Polish resistance. For years, I hoped that one day he would return, that the door would open and he would walk in. I missed him more than I can tell.

Degenhardt led the liquidation of the big ghetto in September 1942 and of the small ghetto in June 1943. He also personally conducted the selection of Jews for work or for execution.

As a policeman, my uncle Felix had the privilege of moving his wife and child to a building assigned to the families of the Jewish police. Claiming his sister as his wife and me as his son, he took us there for a day or two. He then managed to smuggle my mother into the small ghetto, a section of the larger ghetto, which had already been liquidated.

Felix engineered a plan to take me to a building adjacent to a carpentry workshop where another uncle worked for the German army. From there I could escape to a safer place. At an agreed time, I jumped from the first-floor window to a garden below, from which my carpenter uncle took me to the attic of a building from which all the Jewish inhabitants had already been deported. He left me there, all alone, for a few days or more – I lost count of the time – until a way was found to smuggle me into the small ghetto. I found the nights in the attic terrifying, when every sound, every murmur, every bark of a dog, meant a German search party. I probably feared the darkness more than the Germans. These may have been among the worst days of my life.

In the meantime, the Germans searched our apartment in the large ghetto. As a policeman, Felix was allowed to accompany them. I was later told by my uncle that a German found the hiding place of my grandparents. He ordered them to leave, but Felix begged him not to turn them in. Felix spoke perfect German with a slight Viennese accent. The German himself was from Austria. I don't know whether this played a role, but he let them stay, clearly risking his life. After a few days, Felix arranged to smuggle them into the small ghetto.

The small ghetto was in the poorest part of the town. It was established to house those that survived the liquidation of the large ghetto. We moved to a ramshackle house at the very edge of the ghetto, only metres away from a length of barbed wire, which had already been put up by the time we came. The house was primitive, with a floor of beaten earth. On one side of the house flows the river Warta. On the other bank of the Warta was a school for German girls. I could see them quite clearly, wearing

A THOUSAND MIRACLES

Hitlermädchen uniforms. It was bizarre to observe normal life taking place just fifty metres away on the other side of the river.

In the house lived my mother and her parents, and my father. He, with other men, marched to work every morning in a column. They were taken outside the small ghetto for the day and returned in the evening. My mother stayed at home and made rolls and cakes, which I tried to sell, walking from house to house, though I hated doing so. I also had some kind of a job in the tiny Jewish council. It was amazing how quickly everybody tried to adapt to the new reality. Every evening one of the residents of the ghetto sounded a bugle, as if we were in a military camp. I liked to listen to the sound.

One night we were woken up by young men who carried handguns. They were from the Jewish resistance and told us they wanted to dig tunnels from our house under the barbed wire to smuggle arms into the ghetto and enable people to escape when necessary. We were not asked for our permission. They pushed our things aside and dug every night. In the mornings they were gone. My parents were very nervous about the situation, but there was nothing they could do.

Early one evening, I think in June 1943, when I was walking home, I discovered that our house and the neighbouring houses on the border of the ghetto had been surrounded by German soldiers. I could not proceed any further. Neighbours told me that the residents of the border houses, including the one in which we lived, had been loaded onto trucks and driven away. We soon learned that they were taken out of town and executed. I would never see my mother and my maternal grandparents again. After the war I tried to find a photo of her, but could not. I did find two photos of my brother, however, and one of them is on my desk. I do not recall having felt anything when told about the fate of my mother. The stress, the fear, the desire to survive, must have taken over what remained of my emotional system.

SURVIVING THE SECOND WORLD WAR

It was obvious that someone had denounced the Jewish resistance fighters, as the Germans knew exactly where to go. I was told that they found some members of the resistance in the tunnel and hanged them. Had I come home just a few minutes earlier, I would have been captured and executed as well. The rumour was that the executions took place in the old quarries which my maternal grandfather had managed before the war, and which I had used as a playground when we had moved to Częstochowa before the ghetto was closed.

The following morning the entire Jewish population was gathered on a nearby square for selection. The elderly and the sick were told to go one way. We soon learned that they were loaded onto trucks, driven out of town and executed. Miraculously, the Germans let me stay with the younger crowd. They must have thought I was old enough to work. My father and uncle Felix also passed the selection. My carpenter uncle and his wife managed to buy Aryan identity cards and volunteered to work in Germany, where they survived the war.

This was the end of the small ghetto. Soon thereafter the Germans marched us to the Hassag, on the outskirts of Częstochowa. Here we found ourselves in a labour camp surrounded by a tall fence with barbed wire. Hassag was a sprawling industrial complex, with an enormous chimney, large factory buildings and barracks. We were housed in the barracks, on wooden platforms covered with hay, several hundred metres long. There were immense collective toilets and some washing facilities. Food was scarce, in the winter the cold was bitter, and there was no privacy. Hassag produced ammunition for the German army. So I survived, in a way, by aiding the German war effort.

I was made an assistant to three Polish electricians, day workers, for whom Hassag was just another job. I knew nothing about electrical work and could only do basic manual jobs and carry ladders and tools. I suffered from a major handicap because of my fear of heights. One day on a high ladder, I let two high-voltage wires touch each other, causing a flame which burned my left hand all the way to the bone. It was terrifying to see my own bone. The camp doctor bandaged my hand but did not have at his disposal anything to treat infections. The wound was painful but the hand healed nonetheless, and quickly. The smell of burned flesh was actually worse than the pain. I tried to hide the bandage, in case the supervisors should consider me as an invalid, which would expose me to obvious dangers.

Nevertheless, life in Hassag was bearable. It was run for the most part by civilian managers, who were German, with only a few SS officers. One night we were reminded of the imminent dangers. In July 1943, we were woken up, had to dress quickly and run the gauntlet of factory managers, who called out those unfit to work. It was strange that civilian Germans rather than the SS did this selection. One carried out by the SS would no doubt have been worse. I passed, as did my father and other relatives. Another lucky strike.

In the meantime we started hearing from Polish workers about the approaching Soviet army. And then we heard the *boom* of approaching artillery. People were nervous that the Germans would try to kill us or deport us to Germany before the arrival of the Soviets. Then, one bright winter's day, which I will always remember, we left the barracks in the morning only to discover that the watchtowers were no longer manned. There were no longer green or black uniforms around. We saw only prisoners, like ourselves. It was 17 January 1945. I was 14 years old. We had been liberated. Out of the forty thousand Jews gathered in Częstochowa, it seemed that only several thousand had survived.

My father and the rest of the family gathered our few belongings and walked to the part of the town which housed the German administrators. Not a German was to be seen. But Soviet tanks and soldiers were everywhere. I picked up and played with a German bayonet. We could no longer hear any bombings or sounds of war. Strangely, I did not feel any emotion, any elation.

The buildings abandoned by the Germans were impressive. There were proper beds and running water. We decided to squat in an upstairs apartment. In the kitchen we found real coffee and sugar, and in the closets some food. We spent the days gorging on sweet coffee and whatever food we found. There was a hunting dog abandoned by its German owners, looking for food and sympathy. I played with him but soon discovered he gave me a skin infection. I had to let him go.

After a few days, we decided to leave Częstochowa and try to get to Kalisz.

2

FAREWELL TO EUROPE

We travelled to Kalisz by train. It was packed and noisy. On arrival we proceeded to our old apartment, which luckily was no longer occupied by Germans, and we could move in.

Kalisz was so different from what we remembered. Before the war, the Jewish community was quite large, perhaps a quarter of the entire population. During the war, Kalisz was annexed to Germany. Jews who did not escape, as we had done, were expelled east to the "General Government" established by the Nazis, made up of most of pre-war Poland. So were many Poles. Upon our return, there appeared to be hardly any Jews around. And many of the returnees were Poles who had been expelled by the Germans from Kalisz.

When in 2023 I travelled to Kalisz to speak at an international conference, I attended an ecumenical service in the richly decorated basilica of St Joseph, where one of the speakers was a woman who represented the Jewish community. I asked her about the size of the present community. "About ten families, all in all, mostly intermarriages of Jews and Catholics." So that was all that remained of a large and vibrant community. I thought how successful the Holocaust had been in "cancelling" a whole community, a whole tradition, a way of life. And this was the city which in the Middle Ages had had one of the most progressive statutes granting rights to the Jewish community. The Statute of Kalisz promulgated in 1264 by Duke Bolesław the Pious conferred on the local Jewish community liberty of worship, autonomous courts, protection from violence, and rights of trade and travel.

When we returned after the war, there was an atmosphere of tension. The new communist regime was trying to gain popularity by adopting a nationalistic, even antisemitic tone. There was instability, economic uncertainty, and fear of anti-Jewish violence. Indeed, the bloody pogrom of Jews by the Polish population in Kielce followed in July 1946. The city looked shabby and neglected. Resuming our pre-war lives was a pipe dream. I went to school, made a few non-Jewish friends, but felt lonely and anxious. I sensed I did not belong. I explored the parks which I loved so much, but even they looked neglected. I walked to see the place where my grandfather had had his lumberyard. Miraculously, it was still there. During the war it had been under German management. Now, the authorities allowed my father to manage it, without, however, recognizing his ownership. The business took off and produced some income, enough for us to live on.

As the summer came and, with it, the school vacation, I spent more time on the river. The Prosna river appeared much smaller than I remembered it. Perhaps the Germans had diverted some of the flow or maybe my memories tended to embellish places where I had been happy. From time to time I went swimming. My dog paddle sometimes took me further than I could manage. One day, I started drowning and was saved by a person in a boat who extended to me one of his oars and brought me to the shore. Another lucky strike.

FAREWELL TO EUROPE

Uncle Felix moved from Częstochowa to Gdańsk (Danzig) on the Baltic Sea and invited me to visit. I was tempted to go as I had never been to the sea. But getting from Kalisz to Gdańsk presented major difficulties. Eventually, Felix arranged with someone to take me there by motorcycle. We went in the summer of 1945. The roads were terrible and the trip very bumpy and took most of the day. But I was of an age at which practically everything was fun and seen as an exciting adventure.

Gdańsk was still engaged in clearing the ruins of destroyed houses and starting the remarkable reconstruction of the historic Hanseatic buildings. Polish masons were doing wonders restoring the fronts of houses to practically their antebellum appearance.

Of course, the sea was tempting and I spent much time in the water. The beach and the coast were still full of the wrecks of destroyed boats, and pieces of rusting iron were lying all around. I had to be careful, but was not careful enough. I was badly scratched by the rusty remnant of a boat. After a day or two, I discovered an enormous abscess on my groin. Felix rushed me to a doctor who promptly opened the abscess and disinfected the wound. That put an end to my swimming. The motorcycle trip back was very painful.

In early autumn, rumours reached my father that a convoy of trucks from the Jewish Brigade would come to Łódź to search for Jewish survivors, especially the relatives of soldiers. They would be taken to Belgium, where the Brigade was stationed, and then helped to reach Palestine. Father and I were offered space in the convoy. We discussed the matter at length. Father thought that I should take this opportunity and go. He doubted if I would have any future in Poland, and he was sure that his sister Rachel, a professor of civil engineering in the Haifa Technion, would welcome me and make sure I got some education. I was fifteen already, with no schooling whatsoever except for three years in a primary school. Father was still not ready to leave Poland for good. He stayed on and finally immigrated to Israel in 1949. He seemed less unhappy in Kalisz than I was. But I was glad to leave. There was nothing that I found even remotely tempting in Kalisz, and I was attracted by the idea of a new life in Palestine and the prospect of going to school there.

On an agreed date, towards the end of 1945 I think, I travelled to Łódź by train. As we had no travel documents, the group planning to leave – there were fourteen of us, including a cousin and some more distant relatives – met discreetly in an apartment where my distant cousin, the leader of the group, Captain Pawel Mozes, wearing a British uniform and carrying a side arm, introduced us to some of his staff. We were to leave in the early morning. He made it clear that the whole mission was quasi-legal. It was therefore important to choose a route that avoided the checkpoints of the British military police. We quickly understood that the convoy's trip was not quite authorized by higher ranks and that there was a danger of being stopped and sent back, and of its organizers being punished. And, of course, we had no passports or other travel documents. But we had the advantage of a chaotic situation in Poland, Czechoslovakia and Germany, and when we finally got under way, the border guards in Poland and Czechoslovakia were impressed by the British uniforms and trucks and did not bother to question our passage.

I had never heard of the existence of the Jewish Brigade. During the trip I learnt that the Brigade was founded in Palestine in September 1944 to join in the fight against Nazi Germany and was composed entirely of volunteer Palestine Jews. Rommel's forces were still fighting in North Africa and Palestine Jews chose to fight rather than risk another Final Solution. The Brigade's establishment had been proposed by the Jewish leadership in Palestine (the Jewish Agency) and was supported by Winston Churchill. The Brigade saw active combat in Italy. My cousin

FAREWELL TO EUROPE

Zevulun from Haifa was one of its members and he was awaiting me in the Brigade's base in Belgium.

We departed in December, early in the morning. There were three trucks in all. They were covered with canvas, which protected us from snow, but not from the cold. Instead of going west directly through Germany, we took a longer route in a southerly direction, crossed Czechoslovakia, and entered Germany much further west, avoiding the British Occupation Zone, and then crossed into Belgium, arriving in Tournai at the Brigade base.

The trip, which lasted nearly a week, was uneventful, except for hitting a deer in Czechoslovakia. In disembarking in Belgium from a truck in one of our overnight stops, my cardboard suitcase broke, and whatever clothes I had fell out. My embarrassment was great. We spent the nights in small hotels. Our leader paid for the hotels on the way with boxes of Camel cigarettes and bars of chocolate. We were anxious while passing frontiers and checkpoints. Our group tried to make itself invisible during border crossings. Luckily, the inspection of military vehicles was perfunctory.

I had seen Zevulun once or twice before the war but would not have recognized him, especially as he was wearing an army uniform. He took me to the barrack where he lived. We were to share a room. To avoid attracting the attention of the military police, he managed to get me an army uniform, a bit on the big side but wearable.

We ate in a military canteen. I was amazed at the richness and especially the quantity of the food served. I was attracted by the mounds of fresh butter on the table. Zevulun was amused by my slicing butter rather than spreading it on bread. Soldiers showered me with quantities of chocolate, which I was happy to gorge on. Obviously, even a year after the liberation I was still craving for food I had not even seen during the war.

A THOUSAND MIRACLES

Zevulun had studied engineering in the Haifa Technion but did not graduate. I understood, later, that he had fallen in love with a distant cousin, Myriam, also a student in the Technion, but his love was unrequited. She was a beautiful and extremely talented woman who horrified her Jewish family by having an affair with a non-Jewish British military policeman, whom she eventually married, leaving with him to then Rhodesia, nowadays Zimbabwe, and becoming a famous and prosperous engineer. Zevulun could never get over his sorrow and he never married. He was extremely nice and kind. He volunteered for the Jewish Brigade. Manually skilful, he asked to be assigned to a mechanical workshop which maintained military trucks. When I arrived in Tournai, he was settled and content in that job.

In the meantime, my aunt Rachel and her husband Uri had applied to the British Palestine authorities for an entry visa for me, a "certificate" as it was called. Both were very well connected, and it is likely that this application was treated with some degree of urgency.

Zevulun must have exchanged letters with Rachel about my future in Palestine. This was not an easy question. I was nearly 16 years old, with no Hebrew, no English, no algebra, no geometry; a total ignoramus. They all thought, apparently, that some manual occupation which did not require a high-school diploma would make sense. Zevulun suggested that I join him in the mechanical workshop to learn car mechanics. So the following morning I was at Zevulun's side, bent over the engine of a command car that needed fixing. A few hours sufficed to prove beyond a shadow of doubt that I had two clay hands and a mind that refused to understand even the simplest secrets of the combustion engine.

My career as an aspiring auto-mechanic was over by dinner-time. While waiting for the Palestine certificate, Zevulun came up with another idea, one which at least guaranteed a lot of fresh air. A few kilometres east of Tournai, in a small town called Marquain, the Jewish Agency ran a farm cum boarding house for young men and women who had survived the Holocaust and who were strongly encouraged to move to Palestine, to settle on and cultivate the land. The farm was run by a friend and former schoolmate of Zevulun by the name of Bulka. Bulka had told Zevulun that he would love me to join his establishment. Since staying on the military base for a few months was not really an option and would, sooner or later, get Zevulun into trouble, I agreed. So I was driven to Marquain to start a new career tilling the soil: the wandering Jew returning to his biblical sources, preparing to farm in the Holy Land.

Bulka and the young men and women whom I found in Marquain were pleasant and helpful, the place was pastoral, and we were near a canal which, with its ever-present barges, reminded me of Polish rivers. It quickly became clear, however, that Bulka felt he had a heavenly – but hopeless – mission to make me a practising Orthodox Jew. He was very nice about it, but the subtle pressure was clear.

From the first moment, I realized that this was not a place for me. First, I was totally uninterested in agricultural work and found it very tiring. Second, the place was run by a reasonably progressive but nevertheless Orthodox organization. Although my paternal family had a strong religious tradition, we did not really practise religion in my immediate family and I found the obligation to attend religious services definitely not to my liking. The bottom line was that I felt unhappy and knew that neither agriculture nor a religious environment were for me. But, of course, there was no alternative to staying on and awaiting my certificate.

Bulka and his colleagues were well aware that because of the Holocaust I had lost the opportunity to have a bar mitzvah ceremony at the age of thirteen. So they arranged a belated ceremony in Marquain, making me a sort of card-holding but quite uninterested Jew.

The certificate arrived in March 1946. A few others in Marquain received certificates as well. Belgium issued me with a laissez-passer and France a transit visa. The administration of Marquain arranged for someone to accompany us to Marseille. We were anxious to leave and did not tarry. We travelled by train. On the way we had a treat, a two-day stop in Paris. I was enchanted by its charm and beauty. In Belgium, before leaving, Zevulun had bought me an ancient camera and a few rolls of film, so I walked around Paris a lot and took photos of the usual tourist sights and, of course, the Seine. Then we went by train to Marseille. We were taken for an excursion to the old port, which I found fascinating. It was small but bustling with small boats, most of them fishing boats.

We lodged far from the centre of Marseille, in Les Baumettes, an old refugee camp on the outskirts of the city. Years later my wife Monique told me that at that time she lived in Mazargues, not far from Les Baumettes. Armenian refugees had stayed there earlier. After a few days, we were bused to the port and took a small passenger boat to Haifa.

I knew it was adieu or at least au revoir to Europe. Mine was a trip to another continent, another culture, another climate; a journey to a country where Polish would not be spoken; a place where one communicated in Hebrew or English, neither of which I had any knowledge of. Would any school admit me nonetheless? And if it did, would I be able to cope? The prospect was exciting but scary.

3

IN THE PROMISED LAND AND BEYOND

In April 1946, after a week at sea, we arrived in the port of Haifa. From the boat we could see Mount Carmel and the city. There was a lot of excitement in the group from Marquain. The customs and immigration procedures were fast and uneventful. Rachel, my father's sister, and her husband Uri were waiting at the docks and walked me to their boxy little black Ford.

I found both of them kind, welcoming and impressive. Rachel was beautiful and elegant. Uri looked patrician, short but imposing. Rachel spoke to me in Polish, so for the time being at least language would not be a problem at home. Uri's Russian helped him understand Polish a bit. When necessary, Rachel would translate.

We drove to their house at 12 Jerusalem Street, on the slope of Mount Carmel. They lived in a top apartment in a stone building which they owned. The apartment was large and I could have my own room. They had a full-time housekeeper cum cook, a Russian-Jewish woman by the name of Anya. Uri used the Ford for the weekends. For work he had a large car, a Dodge with a driver, provided by Shemen, the large soap and olive oil factory of which he was director-general, owned by the British company Lever Brothers.

To me, the whole set-up symbolized unaccustomed luxury. Later, in 1951, when I was no longer living with them after starting my university studies in Jerusalem, they moved to their new villa in Ahuza, on the western slope of Mount Carmel with a large garden and a magnificent view of the Mediterranean. I visited them frequently for the weekends and particularly enjoyed watching the horizon as the sun set in the blue sea.

Rachel explained that if I wanted to go to high school in the autumn, I had to work very hard with tutors. She spoke to the principal of the Hugim High School, which was nearby. In terms of age, I had to be placed in the fifth grade (the eighth grade was the highest). Given the exceptional circumstances, the principal agreed to give me a chance, provided that by September I learnt enough Hebrew to follow classes and acquired some basic English and mathematics. I was sixteen then and pupils in that grade were in my age group.

Rachel had already recruited several tutors who would come every day, one for Hebrew and the Bible, another for English, and a third for maths (all of which were required subjects on the syllabus). The tutoring started a short few days later. It required complete concentration during the tutorials, which lasted several hours a day, and a lot of homework thereafter.

I faced the daunting task, never quite accomplished, of catching up for six lost years. I was catapulted from the age of fifteen into a difficult young adulthood. Learning Hebrew, English and mathematics, so as to pass the high school final exams, was hard. I had no time for anything but studying. During the months that followed I did nothing but cram. I seldom went out. My company was limited to Rachel and Uri, and I did not meet anyone my age. As they were childless, they treated me like a son. Without their love and encouragement I would never have made it.

IN THE PROMISED LAND AND BEYOND

The only entertainment I had was going with them to the cinema on Saturday nights, after the Sabbath. They had their own box in the cinema, which impressed me no end. They also had a dog, a fox terrier named Ronnie, smart but nervous and excitable, who was good company for me because during the day I was alone with Anya in the house. As Anya was Russian, she understood my Polish and we could somehow communicate.

During the holidays, we would take trips by car, typically to the north and the Lake of Galilee. Uri had to go on business trips by car to Jerusalem and, from time to time, I would accompany him for the day. Cars were still relatively rare in Palestine in the mid-1940s, so traffic was not much of a problem.

Uri was a mechanical engineer born to a secular Jewish family in Baku. His father was also an engineer. He spoke perfect English, subscribed to *The Economist* and *National Geographic Magazine* and was well connected with Mapai, at that time the principal political force in Jewish Palestine; it later became the Labour Party. He had been a young man during the 1917 Russian Revolution, when he belonged to a Zionist youth movement. He loved telling stories of his adventures. Once, carrying a note from one Zionist to another he was arrested by the Tsarist police and swallowed the note to avoid compromising others. At the beginning of the revolution he was a student in St Petersburg. With other students he squatted in a palace from which its princely owner had fled, and spent the winter burning the elegant furniture to keep warm. During the civil war in Russia it took him three weeks to get from St Petersburg to Baku, where his father lived. After a while he continued via Turkey to Palestine. His father followed him.

Rachel was one of the first women academics in the Technion, and was an officer of the clandestine Jewish defence force, the Haganah. She was on track to becoming a world authority on cement. Some years later, she became the vice-president of the

Technion. She was the first student of the Technion to become a full professor there, and the first female professor.

She was born in Poland in a small town called Sieradz, where my father was also born. When she was young, her father vetoed her leaving home to attend the Warsaw Institute of Technology. His mantra was that a nice girl from a good Jewish family should marry and raise children. Moreover, there was an official quota applied to Jewish students, and families gave priority to boys. But Rachel had her own views on what nice girls should do – long before the feminist movement arrived in Poland. Her strategy was to declare a hunger strike. My grandfather was so angry that he refused to speak with her and they communicated through an older brother. He relented only when a physician told him that Rachel would die if she continued with her hunger strike. This forced my grandfather to give in, on condition that she stay in my great-grandfather's house in Warsaw. It was a compromise she could live with. In Warsaw, she joined a Zionist student movement and decided to go to Israel. Her father was against this and withheld any financial assistance. She left for Israel in 1925 all the same and completed her studies at the Technion.

Both Rachel and Uri were patriotic and ardent Zionists. Thinking of them now, I know how disappointed they were that I eventually left Israel and moved to the United States. They did not try to dissuade me from going. I am still very sorry to have caused them pain.

In September 1946, I was at Hugim High School, admitted on a sort of probationary status, depending on whether I could keep up with the class. First haltingly, then more rapidly, always with great effort and without time for social life, I progressed in my studies. Still, my integration at school was less than perfect, as I was the only survivor of the Holocaust in my class and, despite all the sympathy shown me by the teachers and my fellow pupils, I was regarded as a stranger. Three years later I passed the matriculation exams and obtained a high school diploma with grades good enough for admission to the Law Faculty of the university. I was interested in international relations and diplomacy, and the Law Faculty would fit well.

Haifa was a clean, fairly industrialized bi-ethnic city. The Arab population lived for the most part in the lower section, close to the port. The richer Arabs had attractive villas on Mount Carmel, where it was much cooler, and where many of the houses enjoyed wonderful views of the Mediterranean. In the summer of 1946, Arab–Jewish relations in Haifa were still reasonably good, and it was not unusual for Jews from elsewhere to rent Arab villas for the summers so as to escape the heat. I remember one very pleasant summer in a luxurious Arab-owned villa on the western slope of Mount Carmel.

But by 1947 the tensions between Jews and Arabs were rapidly becoming palpable. On 29 November 1947, the UN General Assembly, thanks to strong US support, adopted Resolution 194, which partitioned the area of the British Mandate for Palestine into an Arab and a Jewish state, with a separate status for Jerusalem. Jews were happy with the resolution and demonstrated their joy in the streets. Uri, Rachel and I joined in these demonstrations. But Palestinian Arabs and the neighbouring Arab states rejected the resolution, threatened war and quickly resorted to armed conflict. This was the first time I became aware of the work of the United Nations, which was to play an important role in my later life.

In school, we were encouraged by the school authorities and our families to participate in paramilitary training organized by the Haganah. This involved using handguns and learning person-to-person combat. I enjoyed the sense of conspiracy, fresh air and excitement. These outings were more like scout activities than military training.

A THOUSAND MIRACLES

It soon became obvious that the British had had enough of trying to keep peace between the Arabs and Jews. After being subjected to terrorist attacks, they threw in the towel and decided to withdraw from Palestine. I cannot blame them. On 14 May 1948, the Jewish community adopted a Declaration of Independence and a Declaration on the Establishment of the State of Israel. I listened to the radio when David Ben-Gurion read out the declarations. Everybody came out on the streets and cheered. It was very exciting. History was being made. But the gods of war were cheering as well. The following day, Jordan, Egypt and Syria invaded Palestine, while Lebanon made supportive noises, though it did not demonstrate serious bellicose intent.

For me, a second war began. I was promptly mobilized, along with other boys from Hugim High School. I was enrolled in the artillery and sent to the Negev desert in the south. Here I was not far from the combat zone but was not involved in action. The worst thing in the desert was the sandstorms, which penetrated one's eyes, ears, mouth, clothes, everything.

We all honestly believed that we were fighting a just war, a defensive war, which had been forced upon us. At the time we had no idea that the war was not all that pure. Only later did I learn that the Israeli army used pressure and violence to force much of the Arab population to flee and become refugees, creating an intractable humanitarian and political problem.

Despite the numerical superiority of the Arabs, Israel won. Armistice agreements were negotiated between February and April 1949, with the active help of the United Nations. Israel obtained more territory than allocated under the partition resolution. A large part of the Arab population – including part of the Arab population of Haifa – fled to the neighbouring Arab states or were pushed out by the Israeli forces.

We students were temporarily demobilized so we could complete our schooling and take the exams for our high school

IN THE PROMISED LAND AND BEYOND

diploma. After the exams, our leave ended and we promptly returned to the army. For me it was an artillery officers' school, from which I graduated, albeit with some difficulty owing to my total lack of any sense of orientation. I remember that during one of the exercises, I was told to lead my battery and position the guns for shelling a designated enemy objective. Once I finally managed to tell the instructor that we were ready for action, he congratulated me sarcastically for being far beyond the front lines, where I would no doubt have been captured by the enemy. My talent for reading maps has not improved much since then. Artillery would join the many professions for which I was clearly unqualified. Still, graduation entitled me to the rank of second lieutenant. This ended my military service and marked the beginning of my civilian life. I had no desire whatsoever to stay in the army.

I applied for admission to the Law Faculty of the Hebrew University of Jerusalem and was accepted. So in September 1950 I moved to Jerusalem. The university was located on Mount Scopus. Under the armistice agreement with Jordan, this area became a demilitarized enclave under Israeli control. As a result, access to the Mount Scopus campus for students and faculty had to be made through East Jerusalem, then controlled by Jordan. I remember that one of my early law journal articles was about the demilitarization of Mount Scopus. While a new campus for the university was being built, law courses were given pro tem in two leased Catholic monasteries, Ratisbonne and Terra Sancta.

My immediate priority was to find inexpensive lodgings nearby. I was lucky again. I met two young students, one from Minnesota, the other from Montreal, who told me that I could rent a room in the house where they stayed. It was a large villa on Ben Maimon Street, just opposite Terra Sancta. The house had some history to it. In 1936 it housed the exiled Emperor of Ethiopia, the "Lion of Judah" Haile Selassie, during his stay in

A THOUSAND MIRACLES

Palestine, where he took refuge to escape capture by the Fascist Italian forces.

After the Israeli War of Independence, General Moshe Dayan took over the lower part of the villa with his wife and children; the upper apartment housed a member of the cabinet, finance minister Levi Eshkol. It was a sprawling place, and I had a large room of my own. The rent was reasonable, but the main attraction was being able to live with and befriend General Dayan, a hero of Israel's War of Independence. In the very family-oriented Jewish community, he stood out as a womanizer, causing much pain to his wife Ruth, daughter of a prominent Jerusalem lawyer. They eventually divorced. At the time I lived with them, they had three lovely children.

Dayan, who was fifteen years older than I, grew up in Nahalal, a collective settlement (a *moshav*) to which he once invited me for a weekend. He had been mentored by the legendary British officer Orde Wingate in anti-guerrilla, largely night warfare during the Arab riots or, I should say, the 1936 Arab uprising against the Zionist enterprise. During World War II he led Jewish forces against the Vichy French in Syria and lost an eye. He always wore a black patch and looked like an attractive, perhaps romantic pirate in his usually shabby green uniform or khakis.

Dayan was minister of defence during the Six Day War, which ended in a decisive Israeli victory and the occupation of the West Bank, Gaza, Sinai and the Golan Heights. He was also minister of defence during the Yom Kippur War, which the Israelis nearly lost. He supported the Camp David Accords but resigned from the cabinet in disagreement with Prime Minister Begin. He always gave me the impression of common sense and moderation towards the Arab populations. His English was quite poor, even compared with mine. My first exposure to foreign policy came when he asked me to translate (from English into Hebrew) documents on the Suez Canal obtained, I understood, by Israeli intelligence.

IN THE PROMISED LAND AND BEYOND

In the meantime, my father gave up on Poland and arrived in Israel. He had remarried. His wife had a daughter, Ruth, a few years younger than myself. She became a university professor. He bought a small house close to the little port in the north of Tel Aviv. Once more, he started a small lumber business, which was reasonably profitable. He was an excellent, caring father but I was an absentee son, more involved in my career than in being with him. He lived to the ripe age of 102 and until the end was entirely fit, physically and mentally. I hope that, like him, I will not suffer from dementia. When he became ill in 2002 I rushed to Israel from The Hague but came too late. I have a bad conscience about my filial failures though it is too late to remedy that now.

During the Holocaust, Ruth had been sheltered by a Polish woman, who thus risked her own life and that of her family. Although she received no financial reward from the family during the war, Ruth supported her generously after the liberation. The Polish woman was named one of the righteous gentiles by the Yad Vashem Institute in Jerusalem, as she well deserved.

In Jerusalem, I looked for a job, as I did not want to be too much of a burden on my father. I found work as assistant editor of a Jewish Agency newsletter for its emissaries to Jewish communities abroad. I enjoyed writing but found my boss rather pedantic. I felt good about working, although work reduced the time available for my Law Faculty obligations, resulting in grades that were not particularly impressive.

One summer, thanks to Uri's contacts, I managed to find a temporary job on an old cargo boat sailing to Trieste. It was understood that I would be allowed to take a week off when the ship was unloading in Trieste. I was tasked first with steering. The wheel was connected to the rudder by heavy iron chains lying on the deck. When I tried to adjust the direction gently, nothing seemed to happen. When I adjusted strongly, the ship would change direction far more than I wanted. Not surprisingly,

A THOUSAND MIRACLES

I was promptly demoted from steering and sent by the captain to paint the rusty mast instead. But I promptly became sea-sick and was sent to the steamy kitchen below to wash dishes, an assignment that lasted for the duration of the trip to Trieste and back. In contrast, my time on land was wonderful. I took the train to Dubrovnik, Zagreb, Sarajevo, Belgrade, Venice and Rome. This was my first trip to those parts, and I found Italy especially fascinating.

Jerusalem gave me a solid legal foundation, but I found the old-fashioned educational system, largely based on lectures and memory, uninspiring, if not boring. There was no Socratic method and no open book examinations. Memorization was key.

It soon became obvious to me that I wanted to continue my studies in international law after Jerusalem, not surprisingly after my Holocaust experience. I wanted to be able to do something so that such atrocities did not happen again. And I would not like the Law Faculty in Jerusalem to be the end station in my education. But I needed support for admission and a scholarship to a good American law school. As I had written a fine seminar paper on Israel's acceptance of the compulsory jurisdiction of the International Court of Justice, the principal judicial organ of the United Nations, I asked my teacher, Professor Nathan Feinberg, for a recommendation. He agreed. I applied to a number of law schools and was rejected by all of them, except, amazingly, by Harvard. I still cannot believe my luck that I was both admitted to Harvard Law School and offered a scholarship of $800, which at that time was enough to cover the entire year's tuition for an LLM. As there were severe restrictions on the export of currency from Israel, my father could send me only $100 a month, which had to cover rent, food and everything else. In 1954, when I was twenty-four, I left for the United States.

It was only at Harvard, with its analytical method, that I became comfortable with law, and knew it would be my vocation. The imprint of the war had made me particularly interested in working in areas that could contribute to making atrocities impossible and eliminating the horrible chaos, the helplessness, and the loss of autonomy and normality that I remembered so well.

This was a time when one could still travel to the States by boat. I found a cabin which I shared on a cargo–passenger boat of the now defunct United States Lines. We left from Haifa. It was a wonderful trip because we stopped in Cyprus and Morocco, and I had time to leave the ship and explore Famagusta, Casablanca and Tangier. Finally, the ship docked in Philadelphia in the Delaware River port, and I proceeded by train to Boston and Harvard.

To survive during my first year at Harvard was not easy. I could only afford to eat in the student cafeteria, could afford one new jacket (Harvard crimson in corduroy), and had to share a room in the Ames dormitory with Bernie Fuchs, a first-year law student from Brooklyn. Only a flimsy curtain separated his part of the room from mine. He used to type late into the night and keep me awake. His father was a modest house painter in Brooklyn and Bernie was driven by a desire to succeed. Eventually he became a family judge in Brooklyn.

This downside was more than compensated for by meeting an exceptional group of LLM students, many of whom achieved fame in their professional lives. They included Sheikh Yamani, who later became oil minister of Saudi Arabia; Andreas Girsberger, who later became head of the Swiss Bar Association and one of my closest friends; Thomas Franck, a distinguished professor and scholar of international law who introduced me to the NYU Law School; Samuel Pisar, a prominent lawyer of celebrities in Paris and author of a best-selling book on his survival in Auschwitz; Ted Lee, a Canadian who later became ambassador to Israel and Austria and legal adviser of the Foreign Ministry; and Bodo Schlosshan, who became a leading German advocate.

A THOUSAND MIRACLES

What greatly helped were occasional trips to New York. A distant uncle in the diamond trade, Mendel Zames (he had changed his name from Znamirowski), sent me train tickets to New York, and put me up in a modest but what seemed to me luxurious hotel on West End Avenue. They had two children, Ira and Rebecca. When World War II broke out, Mendel and his wife Hela were attending a conference in New York, having left Ira with relatives in Warsaw (Rebecca was only born later). Hela, in an incredible act of maternal courage, travelled to occupied Poland, retrieved Ira from Warsaw, and took him by train via Germany to Trieste and then by boat to New York. I suppose there is nothing mothers would not do to save their children.

Harvard meant very hard work. But thanks to the Socratic, analytical method, I was comfortable with both studying and exams. As a result of the grades obtained in my LLM programme, I was given a much larger scholarship during the second year and could work on my doctorate in international law. I could also leave Ames Hall and take comfortable rooms in a house on leafy Avon Hill Street which belonged to a lovely Bahai couple, to whom I had an introduction from the wife of the Bahai leader in their headquarters in Haifa.

Two masters of international law – one specializing in humanitarian law and the law of war, the other in human rights – became my mentors and models with whom I worked on a project of codification and restatement of the law of state responsibility. They were Richard Baxter, later a judge of the International Court of Justice (ICJ), and Louis Sohn. Baxter was a true patrician from an old, well-established family. He was hard-working, scholarly, very demanding of himself and his students, and had a wonderful sense of humour. With a friend of his, he would drive around Cambridge in a decommissioned fire engine, inviting us students for the ride, honking horns and attracting smiles and laughter. He was a retired army major, from the Judge-Advocate General's Corps, who completed his studies at the University of Cambridge and became a favourite student of the great professor and later ICJ judge, Sir Hersch Lauterpacht. Once Baxter caught one of his students in an act of major plagiarism from a book by Lauterpacht and memorably joked, "When you copy from many it is research, from one it is plagiarism." The joke did not spare the student from suspension from Harvard. Baxter was a leading world scholar of the law of war or international humanitarian law. His great ambition was an ICJ judgeship. Tragically, he died of lymphatic cancer a short time after his election to the court. His was a brilliant but sadly short career. My friendship with his widow Harriet lasted for many years, until she too died.

Louis Sohn immigrated to the States just before the outbreak of World War II. He was extremely serious, meticulous, demanding. Perhaps because of his Jewish background in the then antisemitic Poland, he was particularly interested in human rights and in the law of international organizations. His optimism and idealism knew no bounds. He became one of the most prominent human rights scholars in the world. He was always a good friend and mentor to me, and helped me greatly in my academic career.

More than anything, I shared the elation and excitement of having made it to the Harvard Law School. I worked hard but was truly happy there. When I returned in 1999 for a semester as a visiting professor of law, I felt this appointment was the culmination of a dream. As it happened, much of my later scholarship and practice was in the areas of expertise of Baxter and Sohn.

One day while at Harvard I received a very modest aerogram, which was the least expensive airmail, from Sir Hersch Lauterpacht, then the Whewell Professor of International Law in Cambridge, offering me the prestigious Humanitarian Trust Scholarship in that university. It involved a paid trip to the UK and what was for me a generous stipend for the year. This was a direct result of Baxter's recommendation.

For the first two terms I lived in Jesus College, to which I had been assigned, in medieval splendour but with a very cold bedroom. There was a gas heater in the living room activated by putting coins in the meter. I used to undress in front of the gas heater and run to the bedroom to find warmth under several blankets. During the third term, in the spring, I lived in the palatial Madingley Hall, in rolling green countryside with a pond, just outside Cambridge.

I made many friends at Cambridge. I also taught Hebrew to Tess Rothschild, wife of Victor, Lord Rothschild, a prominent Cambridge biologist. During World War II he was an intelligence officer. They paid me very generously. I enjoyed visiting their house, which had some magnificent paintings, as one could expect from a Rothschild residence.

While in Cambridge I fulfilled the requirements for the Diploma in Public International Law, wrote my doctoral thesis for Harvard, and submitted one of my first articles to the *British Yearbook of International Law*. Altogether it was a happy and productive time.

I also met and befriended many students, among them Georges Abi-Saab, an Egyptian scholar and later a colleague in Geneva, and Hisashi Owada, a Japanese diplomat whose daughter later married the Crown Prince of Japan and eventually became the Empress of Japan. Both Abi-Saab and Owada became lasting friends.

4

IN ISRAEL'S DIPLOMATIC SERVICE

As I had enjoyed my time in the UK, I looked for an academic position in one of the UK universities after my studentship at Cambridge, but my efforts were clearly unsuccessful. This made me sad. I loved Cambridge and found the Brits a very nice people to live with. I liked their kindness, their respect for privacy, the fact that on a random encounter they did not ask about the origin of one's accent, their tendency to understate. I would have liked to stay in the UK. But that was it. I had to consider other options for the future.

While in Cambridge I was approached by a person to whom I owe a debt of gratitude for contributing so much to my legal education and career: Shabtai Rosenne, the legal adviser of the Israeli Foreign Ministry. He had immigrated to Israel from the UK, where he practised as a solicitor. He was fascinated by questions of procedure, which possibly explains why he wrote the leading works on the International Court of Justice, which focused on procedure and practice.

I was surprised by being approached by such a senior person. After all, I had just finished my Harvard doctorate. He must have heard about me from Hersch Lauterpacht or his son Eli, or from Moshe Dayan. Rosenne offered me a job as an assistant legal adviser, which I accepted. I stayed in the Israeli foreign service for about twenty years, resigning for personal reasons in 1977 and then moving permanently to the United States in 1978, where I joined the NYU School of Law as a professor of international law.

My diplomatic experience started in 1956 as assistant legal adviser of the Ministry for Foreign Affairs (MFA) in Jerusalem. At that time, I prepared for and passed the Israeli Bar examination. Eventually, after moving to New York in 1978, I also passed the New York State Bar exams. I continued as a counsellor with the Permanent Mission of Israel to the UN in New York (1961–7). In 1967–71 I was back in the MFA in Jerusalem as chief legal adviser. In 1971 I was appointed ambassador to Canada (until 1974). After a year in New York as a Rockefeller Foundation fellow and UNITAR (UN Training and Research Institute) fellow, I was appointed as ambassador and permanent representative to the UN in Geneva in 1977. This was my final diplomatic post, which I held for less than a year before resigning.

I have, of course, been very lucky. After the abyss of World War II, life compensated me with so many openings and unusual experiences. Looking back, I realize how good changing orientations, specializations, directions, even entire jobs, is for one's well-being and for keeping young, for not becoming stale in one's little speciality, for experimenting, for constantly learning. Luck or fate is critical for the openings, vacancies, opportunities, but then it is up to oneself to seize them, to take on the necessary risks and challenges. My career choices and writings grew out of these windows of opportunity. The situation, circumstances, needs and institutional constraints were often controlling factors. But despite engaging in different activities and directions when the opportunities arose, I always took on those that fitted with my chosen purposes, especially international law, international humanitarian law and human rights, and the humanization of the law. I always hoped these could help prevent the chaos and atrocities I had witnessed in my childhood.

The Israeli Foreign Ministry provided me with invaluable experience in writing legal opinions, participating in international conferences, and litigating cases. The job helped me to gain a practical perspective.

In 1957, I was asked to accompany Rosenne to Geneva to one of the preparatory UN meetings on the law of the sea. In Geneva I met Roxandra (Sandra) Abramovici, who was attending a school for interpreters and worked for the Israeli mission to the United Nations. We married in 1958 and had two sons, Daniel and Amos. They now have lovely families of their own, and so Sandra and I have eight grandchildren, all of them born and living in the United States. It was a good marriage. We separated in 1979 and reached an amicable divorce in 1980.

Soon after my arrival in Jerusalem from the University of Cambridge, I joined the MFA legal team suing Bulgaria before the International Court of Justice (ICJ) in the case of the Aerial Incident of 27 July 1955 during the height of the Cold War. It was a tragic case, in which an El Al passenger plane strayed into Bulgarian air space during a storm and was shot down, causing the death of all the passengers and crew. Bulgaria contested the jurisdiction of the ICJ and prevailed, resulting in the dismissal of the claim. So we lost. The consolation was that we lost on jurisdiction and not on the merits of the case.

To deal with the case, the team had to travel to The Hague, where the ICJ was housed in the Peace Palace built after World War I by the Carnegie Foundation. We were only three lawyers: Rosenne, our leader; Lazarus, an ex-UK solicitor who worked in the Israeli Ministry of Justice; and myself, the junior. Rosenne did most of the pleadings, Lazarus some, and I none as I was regarded as too junior to plead. This was a bit frustrating, but I was so busy preparing briefs and doing research that I did not have time for feeling sorry for myself.

The court was formal, elegant, and a bit intimidating. We stayed in a small hotel nearby. The Hague was quiet and calm. I enjoyed the occasional and, alas, rare walks during the weekends on the beaches of Scheveningen and eating in the ubiquitous Indonesian restaurants.

Rosenne was a brilliant but not very practical person. He insisted that we open accounts at the Netherlands National Bank to deposit the modest cheques for our daily allowance paid by the Israeli Embassy. The staff of the bank found us a bit strange, to say the least. Our visit was short and a bit humiliating as we were promptly led out by uniformed staff.

After the rejection of our claim by the court, we returned to Jerusalem and tried to negotiate with Bulgaria a possible settlement for the families of the victims. That too did not lead anywhere. I was asked to fly to Sofia, however, to talk to the legal adviser of the Ministry for Foreign Affairs, a Mr Baruch. Sofia, then under communist rule, was depressing. The buildings were grey and unattractive, people in the streets shabby.

The Foreign Ministry received me quite late in the day. It was dark already and the office of my host looked spartan and a bit sinister. I did most of the talking. I was struck by one strange thing. Every twenty minutes or so, but quite regularly, the telephone would ring and my host would ask me to stop talking. He did not pick up the receiver, however. On my return to the embassy I asked colleagues to explain the strange behaviour of the legal adviser. That was simple, they answered: the Bulgarians had antiquated taping equipment and needed time at short intervals to change the tapes.

In my tenure in the Legal Adviser's Office, one of the most interesting tasks I had was to accompany Rosenne to Vienna in

IN ISRAEL'S DIPLOMATIC SERVICE

1961 for the UN conference convened to draft a new convention on diplomatic privileges and immunities. It took place in the impressive Hofburg, one of the grand old palaces of the Austrian Empire. I loved Vienna, particularly its churches, monasteries and convents, its wonderful choirs and sacred music. The conference itself was interesting, and I learned a lot about diplomatic immunities and the art of negotiation.

With two colleagues, one an Italian diplomat, the other a US diplomat, we took a weekend trip to Budapest. I enjoyed its beauty, the Danube and its food. My American colleague, Arny Kerley, a classmate from Harvard, was an opera lover and took me, back in Vienna, to my first ever opera, Richard Strauss's *Der Rosenkavalier*, which is still one of my great favourites.

The Legal Adviser's Office in Jerusalem was staffed with a deputy legal adviser in his late forties and a number of older people with doctorates. The ministry was housed in old barracks at the entry to Jerusalem. The atmosphere in the office was not pleasant, as the deputy resented the attention I was getting from Rosenne. I felt like a change and applied for a post in the Israeli Permanent Mission to the United Nations. The context was favourable, as Michael Comay, a senior Israeli diplomat, originally from South Africa, was in 1960 appointed ambassador and permanent representative to the United Nations. I had met Comay several times and we had developed a good relationship. Rosenne was not happy about my moving to New York, but Comay was more influential and he prevailed.

Thus, in 1961, I joined the Permanent Mission of Israel to the UN in New York. As a representative on the Fifth Committee (Administrative and Budgetary), most of my official work was on the administrative problems of the UN and its Secretariat. I became concerned about the politicization of the Secretariat, its tendency to slide from an international institution (one in which states merge their interests for a common purpose and shared values) to a multinational institution (one in which states preserve and prioritize their own interests), the discrimination against women, and the inadequacy of due process protections for the staff of the Secretariat.

I was on good terms with many delegates on the Fifth Committee and participated actively in its deliberations. Naively, I presented my candidacy for the post of rapporteur of the committee. But I quickly discovered that any hope of getting an Israeli diplomat elected to a post by the General Assembly was, at least then, a pipe dream. Indeed, what struck me in my UN job was how isolated Israel was in those years. This was quite depressing. Apart from some states in Europe, particularly the Netherlands, a few African and Latin American states, the United States and Canada, few countries were friendly to the Israeli delegation. Despite that isolation, I made some diplomatic friends, especially Jean Flihon in the French delegation and Antony Acland, later permanent secretary of the British Foreign Office and Provost of Eton College.

As counsellor in the Permanent Mission I also had some political functions and entertained close relations with the officials of the Palestine Conciliation Commission. I fully reported to the ministry on my meetings and discussions. These discussions involved what appear now to have been totally utopian solutions for the Arab refugees from the 1948 war. Naively, I felt such ideas should be discussed and explored and some reasonable solution should be found to end or at least ease the plight of the refugees. I understood that Israel could not agree to implement UN resolutions granting the refugees wholesale return to their homes, as this could imperil Israel's survival. But that did not mean that nothing could be done to help them, by financial means for example. My reports on contacts with the Palestine Conciliation Commission quickly proved to be an embarrassment for Golda Meir, then minister for foreign affairs, who called me to order, instructing me to cease and desist. The question of the Arab refugees was, for me, placed out of bounds.

Golda was an impressive leader, smart and tough, but a hardliner, and she did not have much tolerance for the exploration of solutions for Arab refugees, nor a particular liking for me. The fact that I had acquired a German Shepherd dog did not endear me to her, as she was afraid of large dogs, which in her mind were associated with pogroms and the Nazis.

I was happy to be in New York. I found the city and the UN quite fascinating. I bought an old dilapidated Chevrolet from a young rabbi who was being drafted for Vietnam. It was a bit incongruous to see a CD plate on a car in such a terrible condition. When the holes in the car became more and more visible, Comay told me that my vehicle was an embarrassment to the Israeli Mission. I was forced to discard the Chevrolet. At that time, Fiat was trying to establish itself in the States and gave considerable discounts to diplomats. So I bought a Fiat 1100, which was nice to drive, but it was a headache as the only service station was in Maspeth, in Queens. The great advantage of the car was that I could drive to Harriman State Park and hike in its forests and lakes. My German Shepherd was a great companion on my walks.

My UN period ended with the Six Day War in June 1967, a traumatic period in which, from the perspective of an Israeli diplomat in New York, the future and survival of Israel were very much at stake. In June, shortly after the fighting was concluded with a victory for Israel, I was offered the job of legal adviser of the Foreign Ministry in Jerusalem – a significant promotion for a 37-year-old – to succeed Shabtai Rosenne, who was being moved to New York as deputy permanent representative to the United Nations. It was in this period that I wrote my Palestine opinions, concluding that civilian settlements in the West Bank violated international law.

A THOUSAND MIRACLES

As legal adviser, one of my tasks was to be involved in negotiating extradition treaties. I still remember a week in Helsinki, when, in addition to discussing an extradition treaty with Finland, I had time to travel in the great forests of Finland and even go to the opera to see Alban Berg's *Lulu*, which was beyond my understanding.

Another task of mine was discussion and coordination with other government ministries, particularly Justice and Defence. These were often difficult, but I managed to establish friendly relations with my counterparts. Abba Eban was the minister of foreign affairs. He was a brilliant speaker with an open mind, seeking compromises and avoiding confrontations. He was respectful of international law and valued my advice, but he was not a heavy-weight in the cabinet, and his influence on government policy-making was unfortunately limited.

In 1969, I led the delegation to the Vienna Conference on the Law of Treaties and took an active part in its proceedings. This was the first time I had led a delegation to an international conference. Law of treaties, like the law of contracts in domestic law, is critically important in international law. It was a great opportunity for me to take part in that conference. And, of course, it was pleasant to be in Vienna again. When I moved to academia, I wrote and published quite a few articles on the law of treaties, even on the law of treaties in the Middle Ages.

In 1971, I was appointed ambassador to Canada, a prestigious position for a 41-year-old. Ottawa was an exciting, vibrant place at a time when Pierre Trudeau was prime minister. I was fortunate to have been posted there in that period. We had a very nice house on a lake where, in the summer, I could swim. Diplomatic life was busy, with lots of dinners and receptions, and I met many interesting people. The winters were very cold, but I was still young enough to be able to cope.

IN ISRAEL'S DIPLOMATIC SERVICE

Arab terrorism was a problem and we were urged to be very cautious. Once an envelope arrived in the embassy, addressed to me. It was exceptionally heavy and our security officer was suspicious. In fact it contained enough explosives to kill several of us. Rosenne had a similar but more benign experience when he was permanent representative to the UN in Geneva. One day he received a suspicious parcel and insisted on it being detonated in the garden. It took the cleaners a long while to remove from the walls all the remains of the chocolate.

Another function, quite onerous and difficult sometimes but pleasant at other times, was representing Israel to the Jewish community of Canada. This involved frequent travel to Toronto, Montreal and sometimes even Vancouver. I enjoyed visiting Montreal with its active theatre life and Vancouver because of its stunning vistas. The job also required helping to fundraise for Israel and promote sales of Israeli government bonds.

One difficult aspect of my job was that my predecessor in Ottawa was now my superior in the Foreign Ministry. He had very good contacts with the Jewish community and visited Canada frequently, too frequently I thought. I probably should have been more diplomatic and accommodating towards him. But I was young, impatient, and reluctant to have a frequent visitor who would breathe down my neck.

One day I received instructions to ask the leadership of the Jewish community to pressure the government of Canada to move their embassy from Tel Aviv to Jerusalem. I felt that this was a questionable request and I objected. My superior was fuming and asked that I be removed from my post and instructed to return to Israel. As a decision of the cabinet was required for recalling an ambassador, Abba Eban raised the matter in a cabinet meeting.

I understand that my salvation came from the minister of finance, Pinhas Sapir, who had often come to Canada and appreciated my work. Sapir, who was very plump, if not obese, once remarked famously that he was on a diet, but plenty of diet. He defended me, and the proposal to recall me was shelved as a result of his objections. Jerusalem advised that I could remain for another year in Ottawa.

This episode left me with a fairly bitter taste and intensified my interest in an academic alternative to the diplomatic service. I had already been taking steps in that direction. In Ottawa, I had been appointed a visiting professor in the common law section of the Faculty of Law and did some teaching. I resumed contacts with my Harvard mentor Professor Richard Baxter and published some articles in the leading journal in the field, the *American Journal of International Law*, of which Baxter was editor-in-chief and of which I would become coeditor-in-chief in the 1980s. I had also published my first book on *Investment Insurance in International Law*. I wrote this book partly to prove to myself that I could write a technical book on international law.

I kept in touch with the Faculty of Law in Jerusalem and was encouraged to expect an academic appointment following my mission to Ottawa. However, there was some opposition in Jerusalem. I understand that a colleague in the Law Faculty objected, possibly fearing competition, and I was told by the dean that the possibility of an appointment was moot.

Despite this disappointment, the call of academia was becoming irresistible. I obtained a year's leave from the Foreign Ministry to go to New York on a grant from the Rockefeller Foundation for 1976–7 to write a book about the UN Secretariat. One of the great scholars of international law, Professor Oscar Schachter, head at the time of the UN Institute for Training and Research (UNITAR), arranged for my appointment as a visiting fellow at the institute. This appointment facilitated my research project enormously as it gave me access to UN officials and meetings. The result was my book *The United Nations*

IN ISRAEL'S DIPLOMATIC SERVICE

Secretariat: The Rules and the Practice (1977). My research also provided material for articles in law journals. The merit principle, the need to depoliticize, due process, and women's rights were among the principal topics covered. Of course, I was building on the experience I had gained as a representative on the General Assembly's Fifth Committee. During that period, I also taught as a visiting professor of law at NYU Law School, where Thomas Franck, my friend and former classmate at Harvard, taught as well.

When the Rockefeller Foundation fellowship ended, I moved to my final diplomatic service assignment, as ambassador and head of the Permanent Mission to the UN in Geneva, which I occupied for less than a year before resigning. I returned to Jerusalem, with my sons, primarily to test how I would feel there, and, after a rather unhappy year, moved to New York for good.

It was for me a difficult, lonely year. My resignation from the ministry was regarded badly and my intent to move to the United States even worse. At that time, perhaps a bit less now, leaving Israel was seen as displaying a lack of loyalty or worse. Even years later, on 4 April 2004, the *Yediot Aharonot* carried an unfriendly article by Moshe Ronen under the title "No Longer One of Us". Overnight I became a black sheep and even people whom I considered good friends kept their distance. The departure to New York in the spring of 1978 was a relief. Fortunately, I had been offered a teaching position at NYU Law School and I began work there in 1979.

5

AGAINST THE SETTLEMENTS IN THE OCCUPIED WEST BANK
MY PALESTINE OPINIONS

One of the most contentious issues of my time as legal adviser to the Israeli Foreign Ministry was the legal opinions I was asked to provide on settlement in the occupied West Bank. My appointment as legal adviser quickly became a baptism by fire. Within weeks of my arrival in Jerusalem, I was requested to advise, first the foreign minister Abba Eban and then the prime minister Levi Eshkol, at the request of the director of the cabinet, whether the establishment of Jewish civilian settlements in the occupied West Bank, the Golan Heights and Gaza was allowed under international law. I refer here to a secret legal opinion of mine, which was brought to light many years later by the Israeli journalist Tom Segev in his book *Israel in 1967: And the Land Changed Its Visage* (2005) and by the historian Gershom Gorenberg in *The Accidental Empire* (2006) and reported in the *New York Times* (10 March 2006) and *The Independent* (11 March 2006).

In this opinion, I wrote that the establishment of civilian settlements in occupied territory violated the Fourth Geneva

A THOUSAND MIRACLES

Convention as well as the private property rights of the Arab inhabitants. The Israeli government chose to go another way and a wave of settlements followed, making the prospects for a political solution so much more difficult. Unfortunately, the only impact of the opinion was that for a short time Israeli settlements were presented as military ("Nahal") outposts. This was always just a fiction. In reality, the government and especially its then Labour prime minister, Levi Eshkol, with the robust support of ministers Allon and Galili, were determined to establish permanent civilian settlements early on, which they did. And it was the Labour Party and not right-wing parties that started this irrevocable and ever more robust settlement policy.

My memories of World War II were of large-scale movements of populations directed by the occupying power. Germany arranged for German settlers from Germany and occupied territories to be settled in territories annexed from Poland. Poles were forced out of Polish territories annexed to the Third Reich. Jews were moved to ghettos, then to labour and extermination camps. Surely, I thought, Jews, who were the principal victims of the Holocaust, would not dream of establishing colonies in occupied territories, even on Arab-owned land.

When years later I travelled on the West Bank, I was extremely concerned by the sight of Jewish settlers making it difficult, even dangerous, for Arab farmers to reach their olive groves, even at times uprooting the trees, which take so long to grow. How could they impose on Arab inhabitants a myriad restrictions that did not apply to the Jewish settlers? How could Jews, who had suffered extreme persecution through the centuries, show so little compassion for the Arab inhabitants?

Although I knew that this was not the opinion that the government wished me to deliver, I had no doubt that legal advisers of governments must be faithful to the law and call the law as they see it. I understood of course that I was dealing with

AGAINST SETTLEMENTS IN OCCUPIED WEST BANK

a critical, almost an existential, question. What strikes me now, when I reflect on my state of mind when I wrote the opinion on the settlements, is that to me it was obvious that this was what I must do, and that the possibility of trying to please the government with some kind of a cosmetic discussion did not even occur to me. In that sense the relationship of legal advisers to governments on matters of international law is different from normal client–attorney relationships. Personal advancement and career interests cannot be a consideration in this context. State the law as it is and damn the consequences!

To the credit of the Israeli government, I must note that there were no repercussions, of which I was aware, as a result of my unpopular opinion. The opinion reflected a commitment to human rights and humanitarian law, and it dealt not only with the rights and obligations of states, but mostly with the rights of inhabitants. This opinion has become perhaps the best known of all my writings.

The first opinion, written in Hebrew bureaucratic language, uses expressions I would not use as a scholar or a judge. But it does not try to mask the conflict between the establishment of settlements and international law. Here it is, in part, in translation from the original Hebrew.

Ministry of Foreign Affairs

          Jerusalem, 13 Elul 5727
          18 September 1967

<u>TOP SECRET</u>

To: Mr Adi Yafeh, Political Secretary to the Prime Minister
From: Legal Adviser, Ministry of Foreign Affairs

 Subject: <u>Settlement in the Administered Territories</u>

A THOUSAND MIRACLES

At your and Mr Raviv's request, I am enclosing herewith a copy of my memorandum of 14.9.67 on the above subject, which I submitted to the Minister of Foreign Affairs. My conclusion is that civilian settlement in the administered territories contravenes explicit provisions of the Fourth Geneva Convention.

Regards,
[signed]
T. Meron

Copy: Mr A. Shimoni, Director of the Minister's Office

14.9.67
To: Minister of Foreign Affairs
From: Legal Adviser
<u>Most Urgent</u>

TOP SECRET

Subject: <u>Settlement in the Administered Territories</u>

... From the point of view of international law, the key provision is the one that appears in the last paragraph of Article 49 of the Fourth Geneva Convention. Israel, of course, is a party to this Convention. The paragraph stipulates as follows: "The occupying power shall not deport or transfer parts of its own civilian population into the territory it occupies."

The Commentary on the Fourth Geneva Convention prepared by the International Committee of the Red Cross in 1958 states:

> This clause was adopted after some hesitation, by the XVIIth International Red Cross Conference. It is intended to prevent a practice adopted during the Second World War by certain Powers, which transferred portions of their own population to occupied territory for political and racial reasons or in order, as they claimed, to colonize those

territories. Such transfers worsened the economic situation of the native population and endangered their separate existence as a race.

The paragraph provides protected persons with a valuable safeguard. It should be noted, however, that in this paragraph the meaning of the words "transfer" and "deport" is rather different from that in which they are used in the other paragraphs of Article 49, since they do not refer to the movement of protected persons but to that of nationals of the occupying Power.

The prohibition therefore is categorical and not conditional upon the motives for the transfer or its objectives. Its purpose is to prevent settlement in occupied territory of citizens of the occupying State ...

... We must, from the point of view of international law, have regard to the question of ownership of the land that we are settling.

Article 46 of the Hague Regulations concerning the Laws and Customs of War on Land (Annexes to the Hague Convention (IV) of 1907), regulations that are regarded as a true expression of customary international law that is binding on all countries, states in relation to occupied territory that "private property ... must be respected. Private property cannot be confiscated."

As regards State lands, Article 55 of the Hague Regulations stipulates that an occupying State is permitted to administer the property and enjoy the fruits of the property of the occupied State. Even here there are certain limitations on the occupying State's freedom of action, which derive from the occupying State not being the owner of the property but having merely enjoyment of it.

In relation to the property of charitable, religious or educational institutions or municipalities, they are treated under Article 56 of the Hague Regulations as private property.

> Regarding the possibility of engaging in any kind of agricultural activity and settlement on the Golan Heights, it has to be pointed out that the Golan Heights, which lie outside the area of the mandated Land of Israel, are unequivocally "occupied territory" and are subject to the prohibition on settlement.
>
> If it is decided to establish any settlements, it is essential that this be done by the army in the form of camps and that it does not point to the establishment of permanent settlements.
>
> * * *
>
> We must nevertheless be aware that the international community has not accepted our argument that the [West] Bank is not "normal" occupied territory and that certain countries (such as Britain in its speeches at the UN) have expressly stated that our status in the [West] Bank is that of an occupying State. In truth, even certain actions by Israel are inconsistent with the claim that the [West] Bank is not occupied territory. For example, Proclamation No. 3 of the IDF Forces Commander in the West Bank of 7.6.67, which brings into force the Order concerning security regulations (in Section 35), states that: "A military court and the administration of a military court will observe the provisions of the Geneva Convention for the Protection of Civilians in Time of War in everything relating to legal proceedings and where there is conflict between this order and the aforementioned Convention, the provisions of the Convention will prevail."
>
> With regard to Gush Etzion, settlement there could to a certain extent be helped by claiming that this is a return to the settlers' homes. I assume that there are no difficulties here with the question of property although the matter requires close examination. With regard to Gush Etzion too, we have to expect, in my view, negative international reaction on the basis of Article 49 of the Geneva Convention. Furthermore, in

AGAINST SETTLEMENTS IN OCCUPIED WEST BANK

> our settlement in Gush Etzion, evidence of intent to annex the [West] Bank to Israel can be seen.
>
> On the possibility of settlement in the Jordan Valley, the legal situation is even more complicated because we cannot claim to be dealing with people returning to their homes and we have to consider that problems of property will arise in the context of the Hague Regulations ...
>
> Regards,
T. Meron
>
> Copy: Director-General

I am often asked whether I stand by those opinions today. I certainly do. My interviews with Donald Macintyre in *The Independent* and with others on many occasions since then make this quite clear.

The Independent, 29 May 2007

> Secret Memo Shows Israel Knew Six Day War Was Illegal
> By Donald Macintyre
>
> A senior legal official who secretly warned the government of Israel after the Six Day War of 1967 that it would be illegal to build Jewish settlements in the occupied Palestinian territories has said, for the first time, that he still believes that he was right.
>
> The declaration by Theodor Meron, the Israeli Foreign Ministry's legal adviser at the time and today one of the world's leading international jurists, is a serious blow to Israel's persistent argument that the settlements do not violate international

law, particularly as Israel prepares to commemorate the 40th anniversary of the war in June 1967.

The legal opinion, a copy of which has been obtained by *The Independent*, was marked "Top Secret" and "Extremely Urgent" and reached the unequivocal conclusion, in the words of its author's summary, "that civilian settlement in the administered territories contravenes the explicit provisions of the Fourth Geneva Convention".

Judge Meron, president of the International Criminal Tribunal for the former Yugoslavia until 2005, said that, after 40 years of Jewish settlement growth in the West Bank - one of the main problems to be solved in any peace deal: "I believe that I would have given the same opinion today."

Judge Meron, a holocaust survivor, also sheds new light on the aftermath of the 1967 war by disclosing that the Foreign Minister, Abba Eban, was "sympathetic" to his view that civilian settlement would directly conflict with the Hague and Geneva conventions governing the conduct of occupying powers.

Despite the legal opinion, which was forwarded to Levi Eshkol, the Prime Minister, but not made public at the time, the Labour cabinet progressively sanctioned settlements. This paved the way to growth which has resulted in at least 240,000 Jewish settlers in the West Bank today.

Judge Meron, 76, is now an appeal judge at the Tribunal. Speaking about his 1967 opinion for the first time, he also tells tomorrow's *Independent Magazine*: "It's obvious to me that the fact that settlements were established and the pace of the establishment of the settlements made peacemaking much more difficult."

Blaming restrictions on Palestinian movement for the devastation of the Palestinian economy, the World Bank earlier this month acknowledged Israeli security concerns but added that many of the restrictions were aimed at "enhancing the free movement of settlers and the physical and economic expansion

AGAINST SETTLEMENTS IN OCCUPIED WEST BANK

of the settlements at the expense of the Palestinian population". The settlements and their "jurisdictions" effectively control about 40 per cent of the area of the West Bank.

The argument that the settlements are illegal, stated in successive UN resolutions, and by the International Court of Justice advisory opinion condemning the separation barrier in 2004, is reinforced by such an authoritative source. It strengthens the political case in any "final status" negotiations on borders with the Palestinians for genuinely equitable land swaps of Israeli territory to a future Palestinian state if Israel is to retain settlement blocks.

Prime Minister Ariel Sharon secured a promise in 2004 from President George Bush that large Israeli "population centres" in the West Bank could remain in Israel in any such negotiations. In a subsequent letter to the Palestinians, the President promised that final borders had to be subject to agreement by negotiation.

Judge Meron's memorandum was obtained from the Israel State Archives. His subsequent defence of it amounts to a direct challenge to Israel's continuing contention that the Geneva Convention's provisions on settling people in occupied territory did not apply to the West Bank because its annexation by Jordan between 1949 and 1967 had been unilateral.

The memorandum was written in September 1967 as the Eshkol government was already considering Jewish settlements in the West Bank and the Golan Heights, seized from Syria during the Six Day War. It says that the international community had already rejected the "argument that the West Bank is not 'normal occupied territory'".

It pointed out that the British ambassador to the United Nations, Lord Caradon, had already asserted that Israel's position was that of an occupier. It added that a decree from the army command saying that military courts would "fulfil Geneva provisions" indicated that Israel thought so too.

Judge Meron also says in his interview that such an argument would not in any case have applied to the Golan Heights, which had been undisputed as sovereign Syrian territory prior to the Six Day War.

While the Olmert government has so far rejected calls for peace negotiations by Syria's President Bashir Assad, it has been weighing a welter of internal advice proposing that it explores talks seeking an end to Syrian support for Hizbollah and Hamas in return for restoring the Golan Heights to Syria.

The memorandum, details of which were published by the Israeli writer Gershom Gorenberg last year, also says settlements built on private land would explicitly contravene the 1907 Hague Convention.

The only implicit acknowledgement of the Meron memorandum – which Mr Gorenberg established also went to Moshe Dayan, the triumphant Defence Minister during the Six Day War – was that one of the first West Bank settlements, Kfar Etzion, was initially called a "military outpost" although it was already, in effect, a civilian settlement. The memorandum said there was no legal prohibition against military posts in occupied territory.

Ehud Olmert fought the Israeli election last year on a programme of unilateral withdrawal from parts of the West Bank – usually thought to mean dismantling settlements east of the separation barrier, which cuts deep into the West Bank in places. But this strategy was abandoned after the Lebanon war.

Mark Regev, the foreign ministry spokesman, said yesterday: "We do not accept that the West Bank is occupied in the classic sense." He added that it was not sovereign Jordanian territory before 1967 and it had not enjoyed legal status since the British mandate, which had the remit, underpinned by the League of Nations, of establishing a Jewish national home.

He added: "That said we accept the principle of two states living side by side and obviously in the creation of this state

AGAINST SETTLEMENTS IN OCCUPIED WEST BANK

> settlements will be coming down. I would point anyone who says that is impossible to what happened in Gaza less than two years ago."
>
> Mr Regev also said that in some settlements – like Hebron where Jews left after a massacre by Arabs in 1929 – Jews had a long history of residence preceding the War of Independence in 1948.[1]

On 21 August 2012, I participated in a CNN programme hosted by Christiane Amanpour with President Shimon Peres of Israel; Gershom Gorenberg, the historian-journalist who was one of the first to access my Palestine opinions; and Hanan Porat, rabbi, educator and politician, and leader of the settler movement (who died before transmission). Here are the relevant excerpts.

> GOD'S JEWISH WARRIORS
> Aired 21 August 2012 – 15:00 ET
>
> (*Music playing*)
>
> CHRISTIANE AMANPOUR: Hello, everyone, and welcome to the program. I'm Christiane Amanpour.
>
> And this week, something special. A few years ago, I had the rare opportunity to spend almost a year traveling the world to report a series that we called "God's Warriors", illustrating in dramatic detail where religion and politics collide and sometimes explode to change the course of history.
>
> Each night this week, I'll bring you these reports on Islam, Judaism and Christianity, because much of what we discovered remains so vital to the challenges that our world faces today.

---

[1] The Palestinian Initiative for Promotion of Global Dialogue and Democracy, http://www.miftah.org/Display.cfm?DocId=13695&CategoryId=5

A THOUSAND MIRACLES

(*Music playing*)

AMANPOUR (voice-over): Tonight we focus on God's Jewish Warriors.

Six days that changed history – the 1967 Six Day War. It put the heartland of biblical Judaism under Israeli control. Hanan Porat wanted to make sure it stayed that way.

HANAN PORAT (through translator): We felt this was the time to seize the moment.

AMANPOUR (voice-over): He and a small group of religious activists began planning a return to the land his parents once farmed, a community called Kafar Atsion [Kfar Etzion] in the now occupied West Bank.

PORAT (through translator): We were returning home and fulfilling the prophecy.

AMANPOUR: But the Israeli government was divided – trade the captured land for peace or keep it and build Jewish settlements? But would settlements even be legal?

In researching his book *The Accidental Empire*, Gershom Gorenberg discovered in Israel's archives these documents, marked "top secret". Written in September 1967 by foreign ministry lawyer Theodor Meron, the memos are a warning that "civilian settlement contravenes the explicit provisions of the Fourth Geneva Convention, which protects people living under occupation".

GERSHOM GORENBERG: It means that it violated international law.

AMANPOUR (voice-over): But if Theodor Meron's legal opinion was correct, how is it that Israelis would build as many as 250 settlements and outposts in the middle of Arab land?

SHIMON PERES: The legal adviser of the foreign ministry doesn't tell us how to defend our lives.

AGAINST SETTLEMENTS IN OCCUPIED WEST BANK

AMANPOUR (voice-over): President Shimon Peres, one of Israel's longest-serving and highest-ranking politicians, initially supported settlements.

AMANPOUR: Are you saying Theodor Meron was wrong?

PERES: I don't know if he was right or wrong from a legal point of view. But he was wrong from a pragmatic point of view. Israel was under a steady attack all the time.

AMANPOUR: So just to help me understand this, for the Israeli leadership at the time, pragmatism triumphed over international law?

PERES: What you call pragmatism was, in our eyes—

AMANPOUR: You just said pragmatism.

PERES: Pragmatism in the sense of security, of defending our lives, yes.

AMANPOUR (voice-over): President Peres now says getting rid of most of the settlements is key to a lasting peace.
Israel's official position is that its settlements do not violate international law. It calls the West Bank disputed territory, not occupied, because, it says, it was never a recognized, independent country.

PERES: The real problem is you can call it pragmatic, you can call it legal. Was the war over? It was not.

AMANPOUR (voice-over): Forty years later, we spoke to Theodor Meron, a Holocaust survivor who became one of the world's most respected authorities on international law. He stands by his top secret memos to the Israeli leaders.

THEODOR MERON: You can justify a lot of things on grounds of security, but you cannot settle your population in occupied territories.

> AMANPOUR: No doubt in your mind?
>
> MERON: No doubt.
>
> AMANPOUR: No wiggle room in the law?
>
> MERON: Not really.
>
> AMANPOUR: Certainly when somebody can present you the Torah, the Bible, and say, look, this is our land, then any man-made law is in confrontation with God's law.
>
> MERON: I cannot argue with the Word of God. Any lawyer can only discuss things from the secular perspective. In other words, I do not believe that the religion can resolve legal disputes.
>
> AMANPOUR (voice-over): But to religious activists, God's law trumped all others.

Amanpour's programme attracted some ferocious criticism from a number of blogs. JBlog Central called it a "most blatantly anti-Jewish program in American television". CAMERA, the Committee for Accuracy in Middle East Reporting in America, called it "one of the most grossly distorted programs to appear on American television in many years". I strongly disagree with these criticisms. In drastic contrast, Simon Rocker, in the British *Jewish Chronicle* on 10 February 2020, wrote that Foreign Secretary Dominic Raab "honours judge who warned against settlements" – "one of the most distinguished Jewish jurists" and "something of a legend". Rocker referred to the ceremony in which I was made an Honorary Companion of the Order of St Michael and St George.

I returned to the question of the settlements in 2017 in an article in the *American Journal of International Law* entitled "The West Bank and International Humanitarian Law on the Eve of the Fiftieth Anniversary of the Six Day War". In this article I tried to answer the arguments of Professor Yehuda Blum and Justice Meir Shamgar, who first developed the thesis of the *sui generis* character of the West Bank and the non-applicability of the Fourth Geneva Convention. In my article I discussed the legal status of the West Bank and the applicable international humanitarian law, and the character of the Fourth Convention as a people-oriented convention. I also maintained and fleshed out my thesis on the illegality of the settlements, especially those established on Arab property. I argued that the time for colonization was long gone.

I recognize that Israel is, of course, not the only state to challenge or reject the application of the Fourth Geneva Convention to a particular situation. The applicability of the Convention has been contested in other situations as well, including – to mention just a few – in Kuwait by Iraq, and in East Timor by Indonesia. In Iraq, the United States and the United Kingdom recognized the status of occupation, but appear to have taken liberties with the law of occupation stated in both the Fourth Geneva Convention and the Hague Convention No. IV. It has been argued that they failed to establish law, order and safety, and effective law enforcement, and that they made far-reaching changes in the civil service. Indeed, the elimination of police forces in Iraq has had lasting destabilizing consequences.

Richard Baxter has noted that "the first line of defense against international humanitarian law is to deny that it applies at all". US State Department legal adviser George H. Aldrich observed that the refusal to apply the Geneva Conventions in situations where they should be applied is "often based on differences between the conflicts presently encountered and those for which the conventions were supposedly adopted". Such denials or refusals with respect to the application of international humanitarian law in the West Bank cannot, in my view, be accepted. Those of us who are committed to international law, and particularly those who respect international humanitarian law and the principles embodied in it, cannot remain silent when faced with such denials or self-serving interpretations.

Perhaps I should explain here, for readers who are not lawyers, what international humanitarian law (IHL) and international criminal law are. IHL is the body of international law stating rules regulating international and non-international armed conflicts. It comprises major conventions, such as the Hague Conventions of 1899 and 1907 and the Geneva Conventions of 1949 for the protection of victims of war, the additional protocols (1977) to the Geneva Conventions, and conventions on weapons and means of conduct of war such as the Convention on Conventional Weapons (1980). Originally applicable to the conduct of states and non-state armed groups, it developed, mostly through the jurisprudence of international criminal tribunals, to govern also criminal responsibility of individuals. It consists of a set of treaty-based rules and customary rules which seek to limit the effects of armed conflicts and to maximize the protections for prisoners of war, civilians and even combatants.

International criminal law, on the other hand, is the body of public international law that addresses the criminal responsibility of individuals for alleged violations of international law, including of course IHL. It concerns itself with the question whether a violation of international law constitutes a crime, and whether an individual may be held responsible for that crime beyond reasonable doubt. It requires compliance with the principle of legality, the fundamental principle being that a person may only be convicted on the basis of legal rules clearly established at the time of the offence. It requires clarity with regard to physical (*actus reus*) and mental (*mens rea*) elements of crimes and gradations in the types of *mens rea*, such as knowledge, recklessness and special intent.

If the continuation of the settlement project on the West Bank has met with practically universal rejection by the international

AGAINST SETTLEMENTS IN OCCUPIED WEST BANK

community, it is not just because of its illegality under the Fourth Geneva Convention or under international humanitarian law more generally. Nor is it only because, by preventing the establishment of a contiguous and viable Palestinian territory, the settlement project frustrates any prospect of serious negotiations aimed at a two-state solution, and thus of reconciliation between the Israelis and the Palestinians. It is also because of the growing perception that the human rights of individual Palestinians, as well as their rights under the Fourth Geneva Convention, are being violated and that the colonization of territories populated by other peoples can no longer be accepted in our time.

I appreciated the fact that in his statement to the Security Council on 23 January 2013, the then ambassador of Lebanon to the UN, Nawaf Salam, later a judge at the International Court of Justice and prime minister of Lebanon, stated that I was one of the first to recognize the illegality of settlement activity:

> Time and again, the question of the illegality of settlement activity was stressed in this council ...
>
> Yet, for whoever may still have any doubt on the matter, let me only recall that one of the first people to recognize the illegality of such activity was no else than Mr Theodor Meron.
>
> A child survivor of the Holocaust, who became one of the world's most eminent international jurists and recently elected President of the International Criminal Tribunal for the former Yugoslavia, Meron was legal counsel of the Israeli Foreign Ministry in September 1967. He was asked by the Office of Mr Levi Eshkol, then Prime Minister of Israel, for his opinion on the legality of civilian settlement in the West Bank, the Gaza Strip, and the Golan Heights.
>
> ... [Meron summarized his conclusion as follows:] "... civilian settlement in the administered territories contravenes the explicit provisions of the Fourth Geneva Convention."

A THOUSAND MIRACLES

Following on my initial opinion, on 12 March 1968 I gave another opinion, in which I stated that the demolition of houses and the deportation of Arabs suspected of subversive activities constituted both violations of the Fourth Geneva Convention and collective punishments. The full opinion was later translated into English by the Israeli NGO HaMoked.[2] I made it clear that the Fourth Geneva Convention was fully applicable.[3] Such demolition would also constitute collective punishment under Article 33 of the Fourth Geneva Convention.[4] This opinion was discovered in 2015 in the state archives by Akevot, an NGO.[5] On 13 March 1968, it had been transmitted to the Prime Minister's Office by Gideon Rafael, the director-general of the Ministry of Foreign Affairs.

The demolition of houses belonging to persons suspected of subversive activities was justified by Israeli authorities on the ground that it was based on British Mandatory emergency regulation 119 (which Israel considered to be still in force on the West Bank).[6] I opined that under the Hague Convention No. IV, the destruction of enemy property not imperatively demanded

---

[2] See http://www.hamoked.org.il

[3] Memorandum from Theodor Meron, Legal Advisor, Ministry of Foreign Affairs of Israel, on Geneva Convention: Blasting Homes and Deportation, to Director-General, Prime Minister's Office (12 March 1968), translation provided by HaMoked: Center for the Defence of the Individual, http://www.hamoked.org/files/2015/1159122_eng.pdf

[4] Memorandum from Theodor Meron, in Gershom Gorenberg, *The Accidental Empire: Israel and the Birth of the Settlements, 1967–1977* (New York: Holt, 2006), 101.

[5] Gershom Gorenberg, "Israel Knew Settlements, Home-Razing Were Illegal", *Haaretz*, 20 March 2015, http://www.haaretz.com/opinion/.premium-1.657167.

[6] See, for example, Brian Farrell, "Israeli Demolition of Palestinian Houses as a Punitive Measure: Application of International Law to Regulation 119", *Brooklyn Journal of International Law* 28, no. 871 (2003), 885–887; B'Tselem, "Punitive House Demolitions from the Perspective of International Law", 1 January 2011, http://www.btselem.org/punitive_demolitions/legal_basis

by the necessities of war was prohibited. Confiscation of private property was clearly unlawful.[7]

As regards the argument that the British Mandatory regulation continued to apply as a matter of domestic law, I pointed out that, according to the ICRC Commentary on Article 64 of the Fourth Geneva Convention, in case of conflict between domestic penal legislation and the Convention, as in this case, the latter must prevail.[8] As I explained, this position simply confirmed the primacy of norms of public international law over conflicting provisions of domestic law.[9] This primacy was particularly important with regard to a conflict between humanitarian principles and internal law. I insisted that the Convention is a humanitarian convention that aims to protect the rights of the civilian population.[10]

I noted that when local laws contravene humanitarian principles, the obligation to uphold local law does not apply – hence the occupying powers in post-war Germany revoked many Nazi laws. When penal legislation of the occupied territory conflicts with the Fourth Geneva Convention, the Convention prevails. Narrow or technical interpretations will not be accepted to exonerate the conquering state from the absolute prohibition upon deportations, clearly stated in Article 49, whatever their reason.[11]

It is a matter of history that these opinions were ignored by the government of Israel. In the years that followed, the

---

[7] Memorandum from Theodor Meron, in Gorenberg, *The Accidental Empire*.
[8] International Committee of the Red Cross, *Commentary on the Geneva Convention IV of 12 August 1949 Relative to the Protection of Civilian Persons in Time of War*, ed. Jean Pictet (Geneva: ICRC, 1958), 336; Memorandum from Theodor Meron, in Gorenberg, *The Accidental Empire*.
[9] Memorandum from Theodor Meron, in Gorenberg, *The Accidental Empire*.
[10] Memorandum from Theodor Meron, in Gorenberg, *The Accidental Empire*.
[11] Gorenberg, "Israel Knew Settlements, Home-Razing Were Illegal"; see also Memorandum from Theodor Meron, in Gorenberg, *The Accidental Empire*.

divergence between the requirements of international law and the situation on the ground in the West Bank became, if anything, more pronounced, with settlements increasingly being established even on private Arab lands, and the prospects of peace and reconciliation between Arabs and Israelis becoming more and more diminished.

6

BECOMING A SCHOLAR

Moving to the United States and to the academic world was a difficult and critical period in my life, both personally and professionally. Fortunately, my appointment to UNITAR (United Nations Institute for Training and Research) made it easy to obtain a US visa, and the Rockefeller Foundation fellowship generously covered all our expenses. In a way, it reminded me somewhat of moving from Poland to Palestine in 1946. Once again, there was a change of continents, countries and occupations.

Of course, for some time already I had been looking for ways to leave the Israeli foreign service and to enter the academy. NYU was beckoning and, already during my Rockefeller Foundation fellowship (1975–6), I was invited to join the full-time faculty. I was forty-six and still a bit uncertain about what I should be doing in my future life. After a short period as permanent representative to the UN in Geneva, I resigned from the Israeli Foreign Ministry and, after spending one year in Jerusalem, NYU became my intellectual home. I found the change exciting but also a bit terrifying. Would my "conversion" to academic work be successful and rewarding? I asked myself.

A THOUSAND MIRACLES

Over the years, I found NYU an exceptional place for encouraging and developing scholarly work. It provided me with a friendly, nurturing environment for teaching, research, and my practice-related activities. It was particularly enlightened in facilitating cross-disciplinary projects, such as my Shakespeare books, which were written at the intersection of law and literature. I continued to write in the fields of international administrative law, human rights and humanitarian law, and, increasingly, international criminal law, as well as on Shakespeare and chivalry. The availability of research assistants and discussions in classes were of course great facilitators for writing. Colleagues were friendly and helpful, and the deans (Norman Redlich, John Sexton, Richard Revesz, Trevor Morrison) were encouraging and supportive, especially in funding research assistants and trips to attend professional conferences. And I was lucky to have a wonderful personal assistant, Sharon Town, an Irish UK citizen, a bright, cultured person with a wide range of interests. Over time we became close friends. Without her I would have found it impossible to manage my transatlantic career. In sum, NYU was an important part of my life, and in a way I am still part of it, in teaching part-time and co-running the ICRC–NYU seminars for UN diplomats.

Upon my appointment to the NYU faculty, the question came up about my principal teaching subjects. At that time, the subject of human rights – the law establishing the rights of individuals vis-à-vis governments – was not regularly taught, although the Law School benefited from human rights courses given by visiting professors. There was clearly student interest in the subject, and the Law School recognized the need for a regular human rights course. I was asked to focus on human rights, and somewhat nervously I prepared to teach what for me was still rather uncharted territory.

Actually, the need of the faculty fitted perfectly with my long-term goal of making a contribution to a society in which persecution and genocide of the kind I had experienced in my childhood would no longer be possible. International humanitarian law had already been part of my intellectual and emotional agenda for a long time, as demonstrated by my Palestine opinions. Human rights, a system of norms which is a close companion of international humanitarian law, in which I had always been interested but which I had had no opportunity to practise, would now become my professional remit. What could be better?

Despite several books and articles on human rights, I was fully aware that my knowledge and experience of human rights were thin. Humanitarian law deals largely with the protection by a foreign government of civilians and combatants belonging to the adversary and is applicable in times of armed conflict or war. Human rights law, on the other hand, concerns the protection of individuals by and from their own authorities or governments primarily in times of peace, although the law has been expanded to times of armed conflict as well.

Teaching human rights proved a blessing, being a natural partner to international humanitarian law. It became one of the two pillars on which my long-term goals of protecting vulnerable populations would rest. The third pillar, international criminal law, would have to wait until the opportunity arose.

Out of my teaching and research in these fields flowed my books. These included *Human Rights Law-Making in the United Nations* (1986), written while I was a visiting researcher at the Max Planck Institute in Heidelberg; *Human Rights in Internal Strife* (1987), the published version of the Sir Hersch Lauterpacht Memorial Lectures which I gave; *Human Rights and Humanitarian Norms as Customary Law* (1989); *International Law in the Age of Human Rights* (2004), a general course given to the Hague Academy of International Law; and its revised version, *Humanization of International Law* (2006), the book closest to capturing the core focus of my work, which offered an integrated approach to human rights and humanitarian law, grounding both in general international law. My 2021 book, *Standing Up for Justice*, represents in a way my judicial legacy.

Over the years, the Oxford University Press became my principal book publisher, while the *American Journal of International Law* became the testing ground and principal vehicle for publishing my articles. Indeed, articles in the journal at times preceded the publication of books on the same subjects. I have been honoured to serve as editor of the journal from 1984 and as co-editor-in-chief in 1993–8.

Once I was established in academia, my work with the International Committee of the Red Cross (ICRC), an organization for which I have always had great admiration, could begin in earnest. It became a major vehicle for my deeper involvement in humanitarian law. While I was active in a number of human rights organizations, my work with the ICRC was continuous and more intensive, and now extends in time to over four decades.

When I was still settling in at NYU, an invitation arrived to present a paper at a Red Cross conference in Hawaii in 1981 on the relationship between human rights and humanitarian law. My work on the paper led me to believe that there was a gap in the protections offered by humanitarian and human rights law. In my paper in Hawaii and in follow-up papers for the *American Journal of International Law* and other journals, I explained that the conventions on international humanitarian law protect victims of international wars, but offer only very limited protection to victims of internal armed conflicts, disturbances or strife. It seemed to me clear that the repression of human dignity occurs in a continuum of situations of strife, from normality to full-blown international armed conflict, and that all these situations must be covered so as to provide protection to human beings.

Moreover, disputes over the characterization of conflicts, such as for example whether domestic strife reaches the threshold for internal armed conflict, create opportunities for states to evade the law altogether. Human rights treaties protect individuals from abuses in times of peace, but many of the important protections may be derogated from on grounds of national emergency. In some situations, non-governmental actors exercise control over people while denying that they are bound by international standards. Moreover, most of the rules on permissible weapons and the conduct of hostilities were not then considered applicable to non-international armed conflicts. There was thus a significant gap between humanitarian and human rights instruments, to the detriment of victims. This was occasionally referred to in the literature as "the Meron gap". As a partial remedy, I proposed the adoption of a declaration of minimum humanitarian standards that would enunciate norms capable of filling that gap for all situations of strife. I was grateful to Professors Oscar Schachter and Louis Henkin, the editors of the *American Journal of International Law* at the time, for publishing the first of my articles on this subject,[1] an article that challenged much received wisdom. I pursued these ideas in my Hersch Lauterpacht Memorial Lectures on "Human Rights in Internal Strife" at the University of Cambridge.

One of the joys of academic law as a discipline is that it allows for give and take within the profession: the chance to use the law, which is naturally fluid, to overcome the stark barriers put up by the academic and organizational division of subjects. Fortunately, Alexandre Hay, the president of the ICRC at the time, expressed interest in my ideas and the first consultations of experts started,

---

[1] Theodor Meron, "On the Inadequate Reach of Humanitarian and Human Rights Law and the Need for a New Instrument", *American Journal of International Law* 77, no. 589 (1983).

eventually resulting in the text of the more normatively limited Turku Declaration of minimum humanitarian standards (1990).

The proposal for such a declaration encountered opposition, however. Some critics feared that a non-binding declaration would dilute existing legal obligations under the treaties in force; others felt that the declaration went too far in trying to impose additional commitments, albeit of a non-binding character. Eventually the project drifted into a deep coma. Since then, the world seems to have moved in the direction envisaged by the project, not through a discrete law-making endeavour, but through the ICRC project on customary law, treaties and statutes, and the jurisprudence of international criminal tribunals, which went beyond the previous rigid distinctions between the law applicable to internal and to international armed conflicts. These developments led to a growing recognition that many rules of international humanitarian law previously applicable only to international wars, apply to non-international armed conflicts as well. All of these contributed to expanding the applicability of protective norms to internal armed conflicts and strife. What happened was a kind of bottom-up transition from the field and from practice to theory. The net result was that many customary and treaty rules formerly applicable only in international armed conflicts, are now increasingly regarded as non-derogable rules in non-international armed conflicts as well, conflicts which are especially frequent and bloody.

In 1990, I was appointed professor of international law at the Graduate Institute of International Law in Geneva. In 1995 I had to retire from the Institute as their retirement age at that time was sixty-five. I also continued to teach, though on a reduced schedule, at NYU. It was a productive and pleasant time, which enabled me to intensify my work with the ICRC. Monique had asked to have her post transferred from the UN Headquarters in New York to the UN Office in Geneva, so that we could be together. We bought a town-house in Grand Saconnex with a little garden and an amazing view of the Lake and of Mont Blanc. On my retirement from the Institute, I resumed full-time teaching at NYU. To spend time with Monique, I tried to fly to Geneva for a few days as often as I could.

One of those commutes almost ended my life. I booked a flight to Geneva from JFK for 2 September 1998. That was the famous SwissAir flight 111 which crashed into the Atlantic off the coast of Nova Scotia soon after taking off. There were no survivors. For some trivial reason, I decided almost at the last moment to leave one day later. Fortunately, Monique knew of my change of plans. We both thanked God. I realized how lucky I was, again.

I began to conduct seminars on humanitarian law in Geneva for young university teachers from all over the world. My involvement in the ICRC groups of experts, including the group on internal strife, on the environment and armed conflicts, on direct participation in hostilities, and on customary rules of international humanitarian law (I was a member of the steering committee and one of the rapporteurs of the customary law project), was both demanding and rewarding. The project on customary rules, which required a significant multi-year commitment, fitted perfectly with my academic interests, especially as it followed my book *Human Rights and Humanitarian Norms as Customary Law*.

With the ICRC, too, I developed and have since co-led an annual ICRC–NYU seminar for UN diplomats on international humanitarian law. This seminar eventually became a flagship of the ICRC's outreach programmes and is now an established tradition that recently celebrated its forty-second anniversary. The seminar reflected my belief that teaching should not be limited to the academy in the narrow sense, but should be directed to governmental officials and decision-makers as well.

A THOUSAND MIRACLES

So my involvement and interest in international humanitarian law continued in many ways.

Over time I also became active in a number of human rights organizations, especially Human Rights Watch. I owe to its head at the time, the extraordinary human rights advocate Aryeh Neier, a great deal of what I have learned about human rights. On his assumption of the presidency of the Open Society Foundations, he was succeeded by Kenneth Roth, another human rights pillar. I enjoyed working with both of them and over time became their friend.

Among the tasks I had for the Open Society Foundations was to head in 1990 a mission of human rights lawyers to the Soviet Union, visiting Moscow, St Petersburg and Kiev, to look into the reforms being introduced by President Mikhail Gorbachev. While developments in Moscow and St Petersburg were encouraging, the regime in Kiev was still very much in a Cold War mindset, and we were followed everywhere by not so secret policemen, making it very difficult for us to meet human rights activists without endangering them.

My principal contribution to Human Rights Watch was in persuading the organization that their agenda must include not only human rights law, but also international humanitarian law. It took a lot of persuasion, but in the end I won them over. Today, Human Rights Watch is concerned equally with the observance of human rights and international humanitarian law.

Here I would also like to mention my participation in the Copenhagen Conference of 1990 on Human Dimension. This was my first opportunity to serve my adopted country. It was an attempt to build on the new spirit of perestroika, or openness, promoted by the enlightened new leader of the Soviet Union, Gorbachev. It brought together states from both sides of the Iron Curtain. We, the delegates, were all excited at the prospect of adopting not only in theory, but in practice, human rights

BECOMING A SCHOLAR

for the Soviet bloc. We cheered the prospect of reviving the importance of the Helsinki Declaration and the fall of the Berlin Wall separating Eastern from Western Europe. The conference was a success. In the Copenhagen Declaration we managed to flesh out some human rights, including those of peaceful assembly and demonstration, freedom of expression, election safeguards and rights of national minorities.

Under the progressive and far-sighted leadership of US ambassador Max Kampelman, the American delegation combined talented career civil servants from the Departments of Justice and State and Congress with academics such as Thomas Buergenthal and me to create a vibrant and imaginative environment. Kampelman gave the two of us prominent roles. Kampelman was also President Reagan's nuclear negotiator with the Soviet Union, and was largely responsible for the resulting nuclear weapons agreements. We became quite friendly and after the conference I came to see him several times in his law offices in Washington DC. He told me that many compromise ideas came up during his walks with Soviet negotiators in the Geneva countryside.

∞

My research and writing have not been confined strictly to law only. In both 1989 and 1991 I spent a term as a visiting fellow of All Souls College, Oxford, following a recommendation by Ian Brownlie, Chichele Professor of Public International Law and fellow of All Souls. Fellows of All Souls are world-class scholars, and while it was exciting to be part of such an exalted group, the company could be a little intimidating. Dinner conversations were fascinating though sometimes difficult for me to follow. We found All Souls not very welcoming to women, or, rather, to the spouses of its fellows. I soon discovered that Monique could be invited to college dinners only for special events, usually once a term. She was not even welcome for tea in the Senior Common Room. As she had a lot of time on her hands, she attended a course on Shakespeare, who had always been her literary hero. It was she who, following a lecture on *Henry V*, urged me to study the law of war and chivalry in Shakespeare after hearing Fluellen's comment to Gower: "Kill the poys and the luggage! 'Tis expressly against the law of arms." After initial resistance, unsurprising for a person whose knowledge of Shakespeare was limited to *Macbeth* in high school, I went to see Laurence Olivier's and Kenneth Branagh's films of *Henry V* and soon became a born-again, if amateur, Shakespearean. I decided to take up her challenge.

Several of the fellows in All Souls were medieval historians, and their mentorship of my new research proved a blessing. And in nearby Balliol College, the world authority on chivalry, Maurice Keen, offered advice and counsel and helped me enormously by guiding me through the historical literature.

If my work on human rights, humanitarian law and international criminal law represented a commitment or a mission rooted in my World War II experience, my work on Shakespeare was pure love. Like most things in my life, it resulted from chance. In 1992, I published my first Shakespeare article, "Shakespeare's *Henry the Fifth* and the Law of War", in the *American Journal of International Law*. The editors were reluctant at first to accept it, telling me that the article was more literature than law. Eventually, it was published after several revisions. It was followed in 1993 by my book *Henry's Wars and Shakespeare's Laws* and, in 1998, by another, *Bloody Constraint: War and Chivalry in Shakespeare*, both published by Oxford University Press. My NYU research assistant, now law professor Laurie Blank, helped enormously. So my interest in international criminal law and in war crimes was enriched by a study of the law of war and chivalry and Shakespeare's history plays.

BECOMING A SCHOLAR

In *Henry's Wars*, I tried to provide a humanitarian lawyer's commentary on the law of war issues arising in Henry V's French campaigns. My goal was to illustrate the law's evolution and show how Shakespeare used the law of nations for his dramatic purposes. In *Bloody Constraint*, I moved on from the laws of war to broader issues of chivalry. My task required an exploration of the values of chivalry that sustained and reshaped the customs of war in the Middle Ages and the Renaissance, values that continue to surface in the legal, moral and utilitarian arguments configuring the Geneva and Hague Conventions and the laws and practices of war today. More than anything else, chivalry meant the duty to act honourably, in peace as in war. Indeed, chivalry's role was not limited to war. It implied an all-encompassing code of behaviour for society. Its legacy continues to shape our contemporary law and values.

Shakespeare, I found, possessed a deep and uncanny understanding of the law of war applicable to this very day. In his nuanced treatment of the themes of war and peace, and of legal justifications for the use of force, and for humanism and mercy, we see hints of issues central to modern humanitarian law and its application. But Shakespeare also demonstrated a profound uneasiness with war and violence. His protagonists insist on the exhaustion of diplomatic and peaceful remedies (as in *King John*), they decry unjust war (as in *Troilus and Cressida*), and, as reflected in *Henry V*, they express scepticism if not outright cynicism about supposedly just wars.

Of course, even today, having rules and observing them are two different things. But Shakespeare's characters go a step further: they show that the justifications driving a just war are often self-serving, hypocritical and opportunistic. His characters deride the claim that war is necessary for the sake of honour or to save face (*Henry V* and *Troilus and Cressida*). They bring into relief the unmitigated horrors of war and they demonstrate the inescapable futility of war (*Hamlet* and *Henry V*).

All this paints a portrait of a man who was not only a playwright beyond compare, but also, across the whole canon of his writing, a powerful voice for restraint, for principle, for peace and simply for humanity; in short, a remarkable humanist.

Academic writings seldom attract attention in the general media. But my Shakespeare writing did stimulate media interest, to my delighted surprise. Tina Rosenberg wrote an editorial, "From Chivalry to the Nuremberg Principles", in the *New York Times* on 23 August 1998 and Marlise Simons a *New York Times* Saturday Profile on 1 March 2004.

One of the more gratifying (and serendipitous) results of my interest in Shakespeare came when Douglas Hughes, the director of Shakespeare in the Park in New York City, took note of my book *Henry's Laws and Shakespeare's Wars*, which he described in the *New Yorker* of 17 June 1996 as "extravagantly helpful" to his production of *Henry V*. Although many productions have trodden lightly around the horrific slaughter of the French prisoners at Agincourt (in *Henry V*), he was persuaded that the atrocity was a central part of the narrative, one that speaks to us even more powerfully today. The *New Yorker* article "Take No Prisoners" by Lawrence Weschler, generously based on an interview with me, discussed the paradigm shift in acknowledging the centrality of the Agincourt massacre. I was happy to make a contribution towards this reading of Shakespeare.

Not being a literary critic, I did not purport to write as one. Rather I wrote as a scholar of humanitarian law with an interest in history and literature. I focused not on Shakespeare the poet and dramatist, but mostly on Shakespeare the student of the chroniclers, of Plutarch and Homer, a humanist who had an acute understanding of the affairs of state and war. Above all, I wrote about a dramatist whose characters articulate a moving call for civilized behaviour, for mercy and quarter, and for moral responsibility, and whose plays are a powerful instrument for illuminating humanism as an ideal for all times.

I tried to show how some of Shakespeare's characters attempt to discourage war through legal, moral and utilitarian arguments, and through irony and sarcasm, as in the famous soliloquy by the Archbishop of Canterbury in *Henry V*, where Shakespeare lays bare self-serving and hypocritical assertions of just war. In *Hamlet*, he highlights the futility and emphasizes the inevitable cruelty and cost of war:

> CAPTAIN: We go to gain a little patch of ground
> That has in it no profit but the name.
> To pay five ducats, five, I would not farm it
>
> HAMLET: To my shame I see
> The imminent death of twenty thousand men
> That, for a fantasy and trick of fame
> Go to their graves like beds, fight for a plot
> Whereon the numbers cannot try the cause,
> Which is not tomb enough and continent
> To hide the slain.

I have already disclaimed any competence in literary criticism. In my books I avoided literary methodologies and their consequences for literary interpretation. But I recognized the historicists' concerns and have tried to situate Shakespeare's texts in their cultural and political environment, relating them to Tudor and Renaissance societies. I understood that Shakespeare's characters speak with a hundred voices and that there is hardly a text that could not be understood in different, sometimes contradictory, ways. While risking accusations of simplification, I found it worthwhile, nevertheless, to derive from those voices certain themes of chivalry which I dared think were probably

A THOUSAND MIRACLES

Shakespeare's own, especially when he departed from the version of the chroniclers.

∞

While teaching and researching, I did argue a few cases, having been admitted to the New York State Bar. One case I argued before the UN Administrative Tribunal arose from my continuing interest in international administrative law and women's rights. In 1990 Jacqueline Dauchy, a French national working for the UN as deputy director of the Codification Division, asked that I represent her before the Administrative Tribunal in a case against the UN Secretary-General. She had expressed interest in being considered for the post of the director of her division, for which she was fully qualified. That post, however, had traditionally been held by a national of the Soviet Union, and the Secretary-General in effect restricted eligibility to nationals of that country, tolerating a "national preserve".

This was an invitation I could not refuse. I argued that as eligibility for the post was restricted to candidates of Soviet nationality, the inescapable conclusion was that candidates of other nationalities were *ipso facto* excluded irrespective of their qualifications. Thus, in violation of Article 101(3) of the UN Charter, which stated that the paramount consideration in the employment of staff was efficiency, competence and integrity, Dauchy was not given consideration despite her unquestionable merit. The respondent, the Secretary-General, insisted that Dauchy had been considered. I argued that any consideration would have been perfunctory, as the Secretary-General viewed only Soviet candidates as eligible for the post.

In 1990 the Administrative Tribunal found that "in accordance with the practice followed since 1964 ... only a Soviet national was to be appointed to the post of Director of the [Codification] Division ... Even the most serious consideration of the Applicant given in all good faith could not have any effect ... The entire exercise therefore proceeded as if the Applicant had not been considered". In judgment numbered 492, the tribunal ordered that Dauchy be paid modest damages. It also expressed the hope that the Secretary-General would carry out his decision to consider Dauchy fully and fairly for any vacant D-2 (director) position. And, indeed, she was appointed to the post as soon as the Soviet appointee completed his two-year contract. The judgment limited the sway of national preserves in the UN bureaucracy and helped both men and women in the Secretariat to be considered on the basis of individual merit, as required by the Charter. Being a counsel for Jacqueline Dauchy against the Secretary-General of the UN and winning that case helped break the glass ceiling which women had to face in aiming for high-level posts at the UN.

One unexpected and concerning consequence of my handling of the Dauchy case was that Carl-August Fleischhauer, the under-secretary-general of the UN and legal counsel who was in charge of the appointment and of the ensuing litigation, felt that my challenging his claim that he had given Dauchy due consideration amounted to challenging his truthfulness. I thought this was not very professional. In any event, he stopped talking to me. As we used to be rather friendly, I was upset. As it happened, by the time I arrived as a judge at The Hague, Fleischhauer was a judge on the ICJ. Monique and I decided to take the first step and invite him for dinner. We were delighted when he accepted. Our relations became normal once more.

∞

One day in 2000, while I was teaching for a trimester at Berkeley, a message arrived from Mike Matheson, the senior deputy legal adviser in the State Department. I knew Mike fairly well from my membership of the US delegations to the Rome Conference and to the Copenhagen Conference on Human Dimension. Mike was a brilliant and highly respected government lawyer, a person of high integrity and professional standards. I liked him very much. He told me that the Legal Adviser's Office was involved in preparations to defend against Iran's claims in the Oil Platforms case, which involved a series of armed Iranian attacks on shipping in the Arab Gulf and US reprisals targeting Iranian oil platforms. He asked if I were ready to advise the State Department on specific issues. I immediately agreed.

So Mike's questions started to arrive, often when Monique and I were exploring the beautiful coastline of California. I had promised Monique to spend as much time as possible touring California and was reluctant to cancel our trips. So I carried in the car a yellow legal pad, so that whenever an idea came to mind which might be helpful in drafting an opinion, I could pull up in the nearest parking place and jot it down. Monique grimaced but did not protest. Back in Berkeley I would draft the opinions and fax or mail them to Mike. The questions were interesting and I was delighted to be of help.

Eventually, following a few weeks of these exchanges, Mike asked whether I would consider moving from Berkeley to Washington as the next State Department counsellor on international law. I was thrilled and excited by this opportunity, but since my sabbatical year was coming to an end, I would need the NYU dean's approval of a year's leave. I called John Sexton, who said yes. He added that it was a great opportunity for me and good for the Law School as well. And so I headed for Washington.

Looking back at my academic journey, I feel that I have been extremely fortunate, and that I have enjoyed extraordinary support from my adopted country, the United States. I think that what drove me in my academic career was not so much ambition and the desire to catch up on years lost during World

BECOMING A SCHOLAR

War II as the sheer pleasure of writing, which is a gift of God. Perhaps my parents understood this when they named me Theodor, which in Greek means "gift of God". The gods seem to have compensated me for the loss of my childhood and most of my family.

7

POLAND AND I

I have to say something about my complex relationship with Poland, the country of my birth. After the war, I often had nightmares in which I was escaping Germans in black uniforms who were chasing me, not catching me, but chasing and chasing, until I would wake up, sweating. In vain I tried to forget. I could not even contemplate returning to Poland and coming face to face with places that left such a painful, traumatic imprint on my life. I did not expect to see Poland again. I probably would never have had the courage to go back were it not for an invitation from the International Committee of the Red Cross (ICRC) in 1986 to lecture at their Warsaw summer school on international humanitarian law. Nor would I have gone without the company and encouragement of my wife Monique. I do not know why she urged me to go. Perhaps she knew, intuitively, that confronting the past might help soothe my soul. In any event, I decided to go.

Even during the apocalyptic times under the Nazi occupation, when Poles appeared threatening, hostile and brutally antisemitic, there were moments of light and islands of humanity, which I learned about only after the war. I often think of the Pole Jan

A THOUSAND MIRACLES

Karski who infiltrated the Warsaw Ghetto and an extermination camp and then travelled to the west to report to the Allies on what was happening to the Jews.

My departure from Poland after the war was accompanied by a deliberate disconnect, rejection, denial. I did not want to hear of Poland or talk of my wartime experiences. I felt embarrassed by my victimhood. I do not think that being a victim is particularly glorious.

I have recently read the moving memoir of Simone Veil, *Une Vie* (*A Life*), and see that my experience was common to teenage survivors of the Holocaust. When she returned to France after her terrifying period in Auschwitz, she too would not, or could not, talk about the Holocaust. And then came the desire to move on, the urge to become normal, to live and to love, to form a family, to bring children into our uncertain world. Eventually she defeated the ghosts of Auschwitz, led an iconic life, and even wrote her Auschwitz survival story.

For our trip to Poland, we used an old Fiat which Monique kept in Geneva, where she lived and worked for the UN. We travelled through the Federal Republic of Germany, Czechoslovakia and East Germany (GDR). It was amazing how empty the roads in the GDR were. We stopped on the way in Prague. Here we found people reluctant to speak to foreigners, even when asked for directions. Obviously, they were afraid of the regime. We were struck by the contrast in Poland, where anti-Soviet jokes were practically the first thing a foreigner heard. The Poles we met were also very helpful and hospitable.

We travelled to Kalisz, Częstochowa, Treblinka and Auschwitz, but also to Kraków, Kazimierz and Gdańsk (Danzig). In Kraków we visited the old Jewish cemetery. We were told that the Germans wanted to keep it as a relic of the past which they did their best to obliterate. In Częstochowa, we could see the building where I had lived in the ghetto. And I could finally visit the Jasna Góra Monastery, and not just look at it from afar. It was strange to hear Polish again. I felt a stranger, a Jewish pariah in a land to which I could no longer belong.

Psychiatrists tell us that confronting a traumatic past helps bring about healing. As a sceptic, I didn't believe that direct confrontation could liberate a person from the demons of the past. Fortunately, I was proved wrong. The catharsis of returning to the venues of my childhood has exorcised from me the ghosts and nightmares of my early years. And these have for the most part not come back to haunt me again.

Treblinka was the most difficult and painful place to visit. Pine trees have grown over the place where the Germans carefully destroyed the evidence of their atrocities: the gas chambers and the crematoria. Only the rail siding where the trains brought thousands of victims for slaughter hinted at the bloody history of this place. This is where my brother participated in the uprising that put an end to this industrial death machine. There was an eerie silence. Trees do not talk. I felt deeply moved by being there and reflecting on my many relatives who were slaughtered there.

Since 1986, I have returned to Poland many times. In 2009, I delivered the Marek Nowicki lecture at the University of Warsaw. In 2011, I travelled to receive an honorary doctorate from the University of Warsaw. Monique was there too as well as my son Amos. The award ceremony was very impressive. We were dressed up like medieval bishops. Professor Maria Kenig-Witkowska of the Law Faculty delivered a very generous eulogy (*laudatio*).

A day before the ceremonies, I went to see the Jewish cemetery of Warsaw. It was very large, all quiet and covered by snow. A Polish caretaker led us to the tomb of my great-grandfather, of which fortunately we had the coordinates. His tomb, like the whole cemetery, was completely untouched by the war. I found it strange that the Nazis destroyed every single house in the Warsaw Ghetto but left the cemetery untouched. The caretaker's theory was that some Nazis were superstitious and afraid they might be haunted by the ghosts of people buried in the cemetery should they destroy it. Strangely, they did not worry about the ghosts of the millions they murdered.

In May 2017, Poland awarded me the Officer's Cross of the Order of Merit, pursuant to a decree issued by President Andrzej Duda. The ceremony took place in the Polish Embassy at The Hague. My friend Professor Elzbieta Mikos-Skuza from the Law Faculty of the University of Warsaw made the principal speech. I had previously been decorated by France and more recently by the United Kingdom, but a decoration from Poland was certainly more surprising and, given the past, particularly poignant.

In my acceptance speech, I paid homage to Polish courage in resisting over centuries forced partitions and foreign occupations. I mentioned that the Poles were next in line after the Jews and the Roma for the Nazi extermination plans. The intelligentsia, the military and clerical leadership, members of the resistance, and so many more were exterminated in great numbers. More than a million Polish Catholics were murdered by the Nazis. The memorial wall at Auschwitz with so many Polish names is a solemn reminder of these lives lost and of the atrocities committed against them.

I appreciated the fact that Poland invited me to brief the Security Council when President Duda had the Council's presidency in May 2018, in the open debate on upholding international law within the context of the maintenance of international peace and security.

In 2021, I was offered an honorary doctorate from the Academy of Applied Sciences of Kalisz, the city of my birth. In responding to the *laudatio* on the award of the degree, I said:

> I am so very grateful to Rector Andrzej Wojtyła and the Senate of the University of Calisia for deciding to award me the University's first

POLAND AND I

ever Doctorate Honoris Causa. And I am grateful to the President of the City of Kalisz for awarding me an honorary citizenship of Kalisz.

This is a particularly great honour for a person born in Kalisz. It is the third honour so generously conferred upon me by Polish institutions. It was preceded by an honorary doctorate from the University of Warsaw and the rank of Officer of the Polish National Order of Merit from President Duda.

The terror and suffering that I and my family members have been through during WWII have been an important factor in my decision to pursue a career in international humanitarian law and international criminal law.

I remember Kalisz fondly from my childhood there prior to the War, kayaking on the Prosna in the summer, skating on it in the winter, playing hide and seek in my grandfather's lumberyard, biking with my brother, listening to Chopin in school activities. Strangely, I have no recollection of suffering from antisemitism in school during all those years.

I am happy to see the progress this city has made, especially with this University of applied sciences, so young with only 20 years since its establishment and yet already renowned for its high academic standards, major research activities and vibrant student community.

Kalisz is of course a city with a long history. Not to mention its Roman traces and its Amber Route nexus, it had a significant development as a medieval town. It may be as much as 1,800 years old, as it was then mentioned by Ptolemy. It was at the crossroads of trade routes and a home to many ethnic and religious groups.

Jews settled in Kalisz, probably as early as 12th Century.

I note that the Duke Bolesław Pobożny granted in 1264 to Kalisz Jews the Statute of Kalisz. For its period, it was amazingly progressive. Its 36 points guaranteed Jews the right to govern their internal affairs. No one was allowed to molest Jews passing through Kalisz. Christians were forbidden from vandalizing synagogues and Jewish cemeteries. If a Jew cried for help in the night and his Christian neighbours failed to come to his aid, they would be punished by financial sanctions.

A THOUSAND MIRACLES

Christians were forbidden from accusing Jews of killing Christian children for their blood, as, according to the precepts of Jewish law, "all Jews refrain from any blood".

The terms of the Kalisz Statute were confirmed by Polish kings and served as a basis for Jewish rights until the end of the 18th century. Alas, they were not remembered during WWII.

For me, Kalisz is emblematic of its victimhood, inflicted by Germany, so close and yet so cruel to its tiny neighbour.

In August 1914 it was almost entirely destroyed by the Prussian Army.

In 1918 it gained its independence and started its reconstruction.

When World War II began, Jews numbered about a third of the City's population of some 80,000 inhabitants.

The proximity of Germany meant that Kalisz was among the first Polish cities invaded by Nazi Germany in September 1939. Persecutions, deportations and executions followed as was the annexation of Kalisz as a part of the Wartheland into the Third Reich.

Many but not all Kalisz Jews escaped east to be soon caught up in the Nazi net, but some remained in Kalisz, to be massacred or deported at first to Nazi-occupied Poland. But although they were the principal target of the Nazi killing machine, they were not the only ones.

I grieve for Jewish as well as for the Catholic martyrs.

It is estimated that about 30,000 Kalisz Jews were murdered but also some 20,000 Kalisz Catholics were either murdered or expelled to German occupied Poland, the so-called General Government, or to Germany as slave workers, making room for German colonizers. The campaign of annihilation of Catholic leadership was horrifying. I note here the Intelligenzaktion and the killing of community leaders by an Einsatzgruppe. Liquidating secular and clergy leaders was a clear criminal purpose of the Nazi regime, cruelly and efficiently enforced.

Most recently, as I have mentioned already, I returned to Kalisz in June 2023 to speak about war crimes in Ukraine. It was on this occasion that I attended the ecumenical service in the Sanctuary of St Joseph.

POLAND AND I

In conclusion, let me reflect on my complex and evolving relationship with Poland. The first stage involved my happy childhood in pre-war Poland, to which I refer in Chapter I. The second stage comprised the dark war years in Częstochowa, which were so different and painful: the ghettos, the labour camp, most of my family falling victim to the Holocaust, images of Germans and Ukrainian SS. The third stage involved total rejection and denial. As I have said, that stage ended with my return to Poland in 1986. The fourth stage is one of opening up to friendship and reconciliation, to the discovery of a new Poland.

I recognize that even during those apocalyptic times, with so many Poles hostile and antisemitic, there were moments of light: a number of Polish Catholics risked their lives to save Jews, including some from my own family. I find it striking and heartening that a country which was as antisemitic as Poland at the time produced the highest per capita number of righteous gentiles – non-Jews who saved Jews.

I came to admire the spirit of the new, democratic Poland, hopefully free of racial hatred and antisemitism, a Poland of which Frédéric Chopin and Adam Mickiewicz would have been proud, and to rejoice at its success in rebuilding this great country.

A symptom of my liberation is that my feelings about the war have become so much more ecumenical. In the past, I would feel pain, naturally, in seeing exhibits on the Warsaw Ghetto. Now I feel the same pain when visiting the museum of the Warsaw Uprising.

I know that in recent years the situation in Poland became less sanguine in terms of respect for the rule of law and judicial independence. I prayed that a correction of the course would come before long. And with the recent elections and the prime-ministership of Donald Tusk, this did come about.

8

AT THE ROME CONFERENCE
THE BIRTH OF THE INTERNATIONAL CRIMINAL COURT

While still working as a professor at NYU Law School, I was delighted when the State Department invited me to be a member of the US delegation to the Rome Conference in 1998 to establish the International Criminal Court (ICC). By then the International Criminal Tribunal for the former Yugoslavia (ICTY) and the International Criminal Tribunal for Rwanda (ICTR), both ad hoc tribunals, were already functioning institutions. I was happy and excited to be able to help in the construction of the first ever permanent international criminal tribunal.

David Scheffer, who was the US ambassador-at-large for war crimes issues, was to be the head of the delegation, and Jamie Borek, an experienced and able attorney, was the senior civil servant from the State Department on the delegation. Other members included Ed Cummings, an expert on the law of war from the Legal Adviser's Office in the State Department; Carolyn Willson, from the US mission to the UN and an expert on rules of procedure; and representatives of the Departments of

Justice and Defense and the Chiefs of Staff. Mary Allen Warlow (Molly as we all called her) from the Criminal Division of the Department of Justice proved effective and influential. Marine Major William (Bill) Lietzau ably represented the Joint Chiefs of Staff in the Department of Defense. He was the mastermind of the so-called Elements of Crimes, an interpretative tool adopted by the Preparatory Commission which provided the legal roadmap for charging each war crime proposed. There were also representatives of Senator Jesse Helms, chairman of the Foreign Relations Committee of the Senate, whose hostility to the project was well known. These were his "watchdogs", making sure that the delegation did not exceed its brief.

The press statement of the State Department spokesman of 12 June 1998 gave a sense of the balancing act that faced the delegation. The United States supported the creation of a properly constituted ICC. In this moment of history, we could shape and strengthen the pursuit of international justice and, like Nuremberg and the ad hoc tribunals, the ICC would hold individuals accountable for genocide, crimes against humanity, and large-scale commission of war crimes. However, the statement pointed out, "we must be careful to guard against the creation of an ICC that politically motivated states could manipulate to challenge the actions of responsible governments by targeting their military and civilian personnel for criminal investigation and prosecution".

My role on the delegation was to help draft provisions on crimes against humanity and war crimes. Eventually I was tasked with helping draft US objections to the proposed definitions of aggression. I also represented the United States in the Preparatory Commission in so far as the crime of aggression was concerned.

We all lived in the Hilton on Piazza Navona, an old palazzo in the very heart of historical Rome. The conference itself was held in the building of the Food and Agriculture Organization (FAO).

AT THE ROME CONFERENCE

It was an unusually hot summer and the air conditioning system could not cope with the large number of ICC delegates. We were all sweating and very uncomfortable.

Monique came with me to Rome. Since she had already retired from the UN Secretariat, she was now free to travel. She had hoped to enjoy a few weeks in Rome, but the heat made walking difficult. Her colleagues in the greatly understaffed translation department of the conference begged her to accept a short-term appointment and help them. She agreed – she could never say no when duty called. It meant that I hardly ever saw her, as she would return to the hotel often after midnight.

David Scheffer kindly suggested that I join him for his meetings with the heads of delegations. I was glad to do so as it enabled me to meet many interesting people. David was well prepared. He had a set piece explaining the US difficulties with the proposed jurisdictional powers of the ICC. The problem, as I saw it, was that he hardly gave time to his interlocutors to react and explain their governments' positions on key issues. The inevitable result was that we did not learn much from these meetings, and they were more David's soliloquies than exchanges and certainly weren't negotiations. I wonder if David's reports to Washington, which I did not see, gave a full picture of how isolated our delegation was.

The Japanese delegation under the leadership of Hisashi Owada, a distinguished diplomat and lawyer and a friend of mine since our Cambridge University days, tried to find a formula acceptable to the United States and the majority, but I am afraid that the US delegation did not help him much in breaking through and may have given him the cold shoulder at critical moments.

Nevertheless, because of the high professionalism of the US delegates, we had a strong and beneficial influence on the wording of the crimes included in the Rome Statute and on procedural and technical provisions. But politically and socially, the US delegation was clearly the pariah of the conference. Other permanent members of the UN Security Council also had difficulties or hesitations about various provisions of the Statute, but the general anger was directed almost entirely at the United States. Perhaps in part owing to the enthusiasm of the NGOs, who were hugely omnipresent, the mood of the conference was giddy, utopian, almost messianic. We were building a new edifice of international justice, and damn the doubters, who would be proved wrong.

I maintained good relations with key people in various delegations involved in the drafting of the crimes, and was, and still am, a supporter of the ICC as regards the core war crimes, crimes against humanity and genocide. But I had doubts about including in the Statute an operative, "ready-to-wear" definition of the crime of aggression. I thought that the court would have enough problems enforcing the core crimes, and that for a fragile and new institution, inclusion of the crime of aggression with its political significance and at the level of leaders of states (given the problems of immunity) would be a bridge too far. I therefore did not mind being the delegation's "bad cop" when it came to the crime of aggression.

At the end of the day, the US challenge to the crime of aggression was fairly successful. While Article 5 of the Statute included the crime of aggression among the crimes over which the court would have jurisdiction, the article circumscribed its jurisdiction until a provision was adopted under the relevant articles of the Statute defining the crime and setting forth its jurisdiction, consistent with the UN Charter.

Such an amendment was duly adopted by the Review Conference in Kampala in 2010, but it has been ratified so far by only forty-seven states – or less than a quarter of UN members. The ratifying states did not include a single permanent member

AT THE ROME CONFERENCE

of the UN Security Council. Not surprisingly perhaps, the Kampala amendment did not help establish the ICC jurisdiction over Russia in the most egregious case of aggression since World War II, namely Russia's invasion of Ukraine. I spoke about this in a conference at the University of Calisia in Poland in June 2023.

But back to Rome. The United States was isolated at the conference not only on the jurisdictional issues I have already mentioned, but also with respect to the crime of aggression. It was necessary for the delegation to speak out, urgently and forcefully. But instructions on this issue did not come from Washington, and Scheffer and Borek hesitated to take the floor on their own responsibility. But it was exactly for such cases that having non-civil service members in the delegation proved useful. The delegation consulted quickly among themselves. The conclusion was that the safest course of action would be to ask me to make a statement, hoping that a dissenting voice might stop or slow down the juggernaut. The problem for me was that I was not prepared, had no text, no notes; the only document in my briefcase was UN Resolution 3314 (XXIX) of 1974 on the definition of aggression. So I took the "hot seat" and spent some twenty minutes or so questioning the viability of the resolution as a source to guide the conference. It was more of an improvisation than a scholarly presentation. It helped to have had some classroom experience.

I pointed out that while the core crimes in the Statute turned on individual criminal responsibility, the crime of aggression reflected on state responsibility far more than the other crimes within the ICC's jurisdiction. It was a leadership crime, involving the highest leaders of a country, such as heads of state, heads of government, cabinet members and the most senior military commanders, and it presented additional procedural and evidentiary issues.

A THOUSAND MIRACLES

I insisted that the definition of aggression must satisfy the principle of legality and reflect customary law. As a "supreme international crime" in the words of Nuremberg, it must satisfy a high threshold of gravity. It must respect the integrity of the UN Charter and thus the powers given by the Charter to the Security Council, and recognize that the Charter gave the Security Council the authority to determine whether an act of aggression had occurred. I recognized that developments since Nuremberg may have allowed its definition of aggression to acquire a patina of customary law.

But the question was whether the 1974 resolution could be considered an appropriate source for codification in the Statute. On its own terms, it was merely a recommendation to the Security Council. The statement in the resolution that the first use of armed force constituted prima facie evidence of aggression was undermined by the language recognizing that the Security Council could conclude that an act of aggression did not occur in the light of circumstances – for instance, the acts were not of sufficient gravity. Moreover, the qualifications that the enumeration of aggressive acts in the resolution was not exhaustive, and that the Security Council could determine that other acts constituted aggression under the Charter, were antithetical to the certainty required of criminal law.

When I finished speaking, a surprising event occurred. Professor Aziz Shukri of the Syrian delegation came over and gave me a hug. For a delegate of Syria to hug a Jew and an ex-Israeli diplomat was quite a sight. He told me that he appreciated the fact that I did not make my statement a vehicle for attacking Arabs. As a postscript to this, when the US nominated me for an ICTY judgeship in 2001, Syria was among the first states to promise support.

The other notable event was that right after my speech, the very impressive head of the UK delegation, Frank Berman, who

AT THE ROME CONFERENCE

was sitting next to me when I was in the hot seat, made a strong statement against the definition of aggression, thus encouraging others to take a sceptical line.

In a more formal statement, during the Preparatory Commission, I emphasized that the ICC should codify existing customary law and not establish new law.

> We remain unconvinced that the Resolution states customary law for purposes of international criminal law, for the crime of aggression.
>
> At the time of its adoption, the Resolution did not ... restate already existing customary international law.
>
> Of course, a resolution could become customary law subsequent to its adoption. A resolution could become a focal point of a subsequent practice of states and harden into customary law ...
>
> But, as the [International Court of Justice] taught us time and again, for this kind of transformation, two requirements have to be complied with. You have to have concordant settled practice and you have to have *opinio juris generalis* [a state's sense of obligation to follow a customary international law]. In the words of the North Sea Continental Shelf cases, one has to demonstrate a settled practice and evidence of a belief that the practice is obligatory by the existence of a rule of law requiring it. Or, as the Nicaragua judgment stated, the existence of a rule in the *opinio juris* of states must be confirmed in practice.
>
> Obviously, there has been no concordant practice based on the General Assembly Resolution on the definition of aggression. Just look at the records of the Security Council. And if anyone still had any doubts, the controversy in our own discussions has clearly demonstrated the absence of *opinio juris generalis*.

Almost six weeks of negotiations had not produced an agreed Statute text. Facing a possible failure, the president of the conference convened a small group of delegates to draft a text, which was circulated to the delegations as the deadline approached. With time running out, the final assembly convened, and in the early morning hours (3 am, I think) the vote, which was not recorded, was taken. There was silence in the room when the United States voted no.

And thus, on 17 July 1998, the Rome Conference adopted the Rome Statute of the ICC by a vote of 121 to 7, with 21 abstentions. There was tremendous applause and much enthusiasm. Among delegates there was a sense of triumphalism that the Statute had been adopted by such a great majority and some satisfaction that the United States had lost. Everybody blamed us.

I thought of Charles Dickens' line in the opening paragraph of *A Tale of Two Cities*: "It was the best of times, it was the worst of times." For me and the US delegation, it was the worst of times. I had never felt so much of a pariah as at that moment. But I also felt happy that the Statute had been adopted, though I was glad that the conference was over.

9

IN THE US STATE DEPARTMENT
THE UPS AND DOWNS OF A JUDICIAL NOMINATION

In 2001–2 I worked in Washington DC at the State Department as counsellor on international law. This job gave me a high profile, an insider's network, and thus a unique opportunity to be considered for a UN war crimes judgeship.

I felt deeply about the war crimes that were committed in the former Yugoslavia, the killings, the ethnic cleansing, the mass rapes. And I was shocked by the genocide committed in Rwanda by Hutus against Tutsis. I found these not only shocking but painful reminders of my years in Poland during World War II.

My life in Washington DC was a happy one. Monique was with me the whole of the time. We rented a house in northern DC. We bought a car and could explore on weekends the coasts of Chesapeake Bay and the Blue Mountains, and hike along the Chesapeake & Ohio Canal and the Potomac River. Colleagues in the Legal Adviser's Office in the State Department often invited us for dinners, and we made some lasting friendships. As my son Dan lived in the nearby town of Potomac, we could see him and his family fairly often.

A THOUSAND MIRACLES

At the State Department I was involved in negotiations, litigation and advising. As counsellor, I was considered part of the front office and participated in morning meetings of the legal adviser or the acting legal adviser and his deputies. I made myself particularly available to the younger attorneys, who often sought my advice and suggestions and who quickly learned that their discussions with me would remain confidential. This was important as I knew that young attorneys were often reluctant to ask questions in the presence of more senior colleagues. I was impressed by the professionalism and collegiality of those who worked with me. Of course, because of my past work in the Israeli diplomatic service, I recused myself from anything to do with Israel.

Sometime in 2000 it became known that Patricia Wald, past senior judge in the District of Columbia Federal Court, would not seek re-election to her current post as a judge of the International Criminal Tribunal for the former Yugoslavia when her term was due to expire on 6 November 2001, because of her husband's health problems.

About a year earlier, on 10 November 2000, the UN Secretary-General requested member states to submit nominations for judgeships in the ICTY within sixty days. The State Department accordingly invited interested persons to submit their candidatures. The Legal Adviser's Office was in charge of this process, as was the practice for nominations of judges to international criminal tribunals. Jim Thessin, the senior deputy legal adviser and a specialist in professional ethics, was the acting legal adviser responsible for the file. Only much later I learnt that he had been assisted by Stephen Mathias, assistant legal adviser for UN affairs, already a rising star in the office and now assistant secretary-general and deputy legal counsel of the United Nations.

By then I had established a certain reputation in the field of international criminal law. In 1993 I authored an article in *Foreign*

IN THE US STATE DEPARTMENT

Affairs magazine, stating the case for establishing a criminal tribunal to prosecute war crimes in the former Yugoslavia, which grew out of my role as rapporteur of an informal working group led by Ambassador Rita Hauser of the Council on Foreign Relations. That year I also published an article in the *American Journal of International Law* urging reforms in what were then inadequate international law prohibitions of rape. I advised Justice Richard Goldstone, the prosecutor of the ICTY, and his team in the Tadić interlocutory appeal in 1995. This resulted in a landmark decision of Judge Antonio Cassese determining that most of the protective provisions of international humanitarian law governing international armed conflicts were applicable in non-international armed conflicts as well. In 1998, as I have outlined in the previous chapter, I was a member of the US delegation to the Rome Conference convened to establish the International Criminal Court (ICC). As counsellor on international law in the State Department, I was frequently consulted on international criminal law and on the jurisdiction of the ICC. Given that background, I decided to submit my candidature to the selection committee for an ICTY judgeship.

For me, a survivor and a victim of the Holocaust and an international lawyer many of whose family members were killed by the Nazis, not to try to seize the opportunity to become a UN war crimes judge would have been morally unacceptable. I was convinced that if selected, I would judge justly and fairly, without fear or favour.

Of course, I did not know for certain who the other candidates were. It was an open secret, however, that one candidate was David Scheffer, ambassador-at-large for war crimes under Secretary of State Madeleine Albright and her adviser when she was US permanent representative to the United Nations. Scheffer was a nice, personable and hard-working person, whose principal activity was to seek the arrests of persons indicted by the ICTY and the ICTR and secure their delivery for trial at The Hague or in Arusha. This proved to be one of his weak points for the appointment that he was seeking. The very influential Office of the Legal Adviser feared that Scheffer's activities might compel him to recuse himself from many cases if he became a judge.

I still recall an evening in November 2000 when I stayed late at work, as I had some papers to finish. George W. Bush had just been elected US president; David Andrews, the Clinton-appointed legal adviser of the State Department had already left Washington DC; and William Taft, the nominee for that post, would still need to be confirmed by the Senate as the new administration bedded down. In short, there was no legal adviser at that time in the State Department. As a result, during this interregnum, I was given the empty office of the legal adviser, following the tradition that neither the civil service acting legal adviser nor the unconfirmed nominee would use the office, thus avoiding any undesirable expectations or appearances. I was thus happily ensconced in the room of the legal adviser, far above my station. It was very large and elegantly furnished, with an en suite toilet and shower. Since I did not ask for it but had been assigned to it, my conscience was clear.

That evening proved anything but routine. The acting legal adviser, Jim Thessin, came back from his meeting with the Secretary of State in her office on the seventh floor. He entered "my" office on the sixth floor, obviously upset and angry. He was always a courteous, calm and much-respected civil servant, a pious Catholic, and this was the first time that I had heard him swear. "Look at what she did to our report," he shouted. He showed me the document. This was the first time I had seen it. The report contained five names: Scheffer of course, two federal district judges, a prominent female academic from a leading law school, and me. Each name was accompanied by an explanatory paragraph. Then there was a summary and, as is customary for

IN THE US STATE DEPARTMENT

such reports, a final recommendation of a single individual. I was the recommended person.

I now understood why Jim was angry. My name had been crossed out by Secretary Albright. Instead, she wrote in her neat handwriting: "I nominate David Scheffer."

SENSITIVE BUT UNCLASSIFIED

- 6 -

international humanitarian law and international law. By virtue of his current service as Counselor on International Law, his views on the relevant issues are known to the Department. We believe that, by virtue of his expertise and reputation, he would be well-suited to play a major role at the Tribunal in the sound development of the Tribunal's jurisprudence.

Ambassador Scheffer's personal and professional commitment to the ICTY is unquestionable, and he, too, is well-known internationally in the international humanitarian law area, primarily in his capacity as a U.S. Government official. His views on the development of international humanitarian law and such international legal issues as the relationship between the Tribunal and States are also known to the Department. While Ambassador Scheffer is highly qualified to serve as a judge on the Tribunal, we are concerned that, because of his activities as Ambassador-at-large, he may have to recuse himself in some of the Tribunal's most significant cases and that this may impair his effectiveness as a judge of the Tribunal.

Professor Wedgwood enjoys an excellent reputation internationally and is increasingly associated with professional writings in the area of international criminal law. Her views on the future direction of the development of international humanitarian law and such questions as the Tribunal's appropriate relationship with States are not fully known to the Department.

RECOMMENDATION

That you designate Theoder Meron as the nominee of the United States for Judge on the International Criminal Tribunal for the Former Yugoslavia.

Approve _____   Disapprove ✓ MKA 01/08/01

I nominate David Scheffer -

SENSITIVE BUT UNCLASSIFIED

A THOUSAND MIRACLES

No discussion, no referral to the Office of the Legal Adviser, just a clear executive decision, which was surely within the Secretary's authority although it may have been a questionable process. I, for one, have always felt that not following normal processes is always dangerous; it simply does not seem right. I was disappointed, sad, but that was it. My short march to glory was over.

A few days later Scheffer called to tell me that the Secretary had nominated him for the judgeship. I was angry because he presented the matter as if it were only her decision, which in a way was true, and that he was not involved, which I doubted. I hung up on him and later regretted my action. After all, life is competitive, and he was the winner. I should have respected the outcome.

Years later, Madeleine Albright came on a visit to The Hague and I was invited to an official function which involved a dinner with her. As president of the tribunal, I was seated next to her. She involved me in a conversation about The Hague, and said nothing about the Scheffer incident, and altogether she was absolutely nice, even charming. I wondered whether she felt a tiny bit uncomfortable about what she had done to the report of the legal adviser's selection committee and thus to me. I will never know.

The letter of the UN Secretary-General had asked states to submit nominations for ICTY judges by 9 January 2001. The US mission submitted Scheffer's nomination on time. There was no room for further nominations. As they say at the roulette table, *rien ne va plus* – no further bets. End of story.

But not quite. Ukraine, a member of the Security Council, realized belatedly that it had missed submitting a Ukrainian candidate in time and requested the Council to grant an extension. Of course, the Council could not grant such an extension to a single state, so the extension until 31 January was granted to all.

IN THE US STATE DEPARTMENT

The second development was that the new US administration came into office. Colin Powell was the new Secretary of State, and, according to rumours, the last thing he wanted to do was to antagonize Madeleine Albright by reopening the ICTY appointment process. However, the new administration heard what had happened and had no interest in maintaining Albright's decision. The inclination to reopen the matter was supported by the dissatisfaction of the civil service in the State Department with the way the nomination had been handled by Albright.

At the time I was aware of the anger that her decision triggered in the Legal Adviser's Office, but I was not aware of any wider dissatisfaction. This was partly because I was preparing for a mission to Montreux to discuss new proposals by the International Committee of the Red Cross (ICRC) for assessing the legality of certain weapons systems which routinely caused superfluous injury or unnecessary suffering. Eventually, this project went nowhere largely because of the opposition of the United States and, I suspect, some other big powers.

As Powell was reluctant to reopen the nomination for judges, he did so only after repeated and insistent orders from the president's chief of staff, Andy Card, on behalf of the president. The orders from the White House apparently were not to reverse the decision of Albright per se but to look at the matter again. Once the whole story became known to the Secretary and to the White House, however, Powell yielded and ordered the State Department to withdraw Scheffer's nomination and substitute my own.

As with most things in Washington DC, some people must have leaked to the press the story of my demise as a candidate for a judgeship. On 29 January, Al Kamen in his widely read column "In the Loop" in the *Washington Post* wrote:

> Looked like a seat on the International Criminal Tribunal in The Hague was all set for former secretary of state Madeleine K. Albright's

pick, David J. Scheffer, ambassador at large for war crimes issues. But the UN Security Council vote on the nomination has been delayed to Wednesday, and some folks in the legal and European bureaus want Secretary of State Colin L. Powell to sub New York University international law professor Theodor Meron for the job.

It was actually on 8 February that the Security Council decided to transmit to the General Assembly a list of candidates for the Assembly's consideration. It included my, and no longer Scheffer's, nomination. Then things started moving rapidly in Washington DC. I was then in Montreux, still in blissful ignorance of developments in the capital. The last day of January was the deadline for the submission of nominations. This deadline was almost missed perhaps because of the reluctance of Powell to override Albright. In any event, on the evening of 31 January I was in Montreux, where I was having a loud and cheerful dinner with my colleagues on the US delegation in a downtown pizzeria.

Strange things started happening. David Kaye, the very effective special adviser of the acting legal adviser, called to ask whether I had any criminal convictions. He did not explain why he asked the question. I said, of course, no. An hour later another call came from him. Did I have any nationalities apart from that of the United States? As I had renounced my Israeli nationality in the 1980s, no again. I started to think this must be relevant to the ICTY nominations.

We then drove back to our hotel on the mountain, which had a fabulous view of Lake Geneva below and the snow-covered Alps beyond. As I was falling asleep, I had a call from Jim Thessin. He wanted to congratulate me. Secretary Powell had decided to nominate me and a telegram instructing the US mission to the UN had just been sent. Carolyn Willson was making sure that someone in the Secretariat would wait for her to receive the

The author, then aged five, with his older brother, who died at the age of seventeen while taking part in the prisoners' uprising in Treblinka.

On the river in Kalisz before the war.

In Palestine, 1945.

The author with fellow judges in Arusha.

At the podium of the UN General Assembly.

With Red Cross delegates in Abu Dhabi.

Official portrait of the author as a UN war crimes judge.

At All Souls College, Oxford.

Monique and I with some of my law clerks.

With the rector of
Kalisia University.

The author visiting the memorial to the victims of the Srebrenica genocide. Photo © Amel Emric.

The author's father at his 100th birthday party with his sons and grandchildren.

Monique.

Tree planted in a garden of Trinity College, Oxford in memory of Monique.

IN THE US STATE DEPARTMENT

nomination document. The change of nominees had to be done before the midnight deadline or would not happen at all.

So I won this one. But there was no triumphal element in this. There were no good guys or bad guys in what happened. There was just a difficult situation for everybody concerned. David Scheffer had as good a claim for nomination as I did. Albright was within her rights in overriding the committee's recommendation. But Tyche, the Greek goddess of fortune and luck, was clearly on my side this time, tilting the scale. Her role is gratefully acknowledged. And I am grateful to all those in the State Department who did not approve of what the Secretary of State had done and advocated the restoration of the original recommendation.

But being a candidate did not mean that I would have the vote of the absolute majority of the UN. For that I would need at least some Arab and Muslim support. It would have helped if my Palestinian opinions had been unearthed by then. But they were discovered in the Israeli state archives only four or five years later, in 2005–6.

I was fairly well known in the UN because of my role in the Rome Conference, my books and articles, and my role in co-leading the annual ICRC–NYU seminars on international humanitarian law for UN diplomats. But this was not necessarily enough, and I worried about the outcome. To say the least, being a Jew and an ex-Israeli diplomat was a bit of a problem.

Again Tyche showed her benevolence. Ambassador Ahmed Aboul Gheit was the permanent representative of Egypt to the UN in 2001. Soon thereafter he became the foreign minister of Egypt. My election officer and friend, Carolyn Willson, knew him well and arranged for me to meet him.

Of course I came to the UN to lobby diplomats, as all the candidates did. The meetings were held in the delegates' lounge or in the Indonesian lounge in the UN building. The object was to make them know me and hopefully vote for me. Carolyn and I carried with us a tiny US flag, which we would put on the table we used for the meeting. I still keep this flag on my desk. In these meetings, the candidate would try to impress the diplomats with his legal qualifications. But the meeting with the Egyptian was different. He had read about me and my personal history and concluded that someone with my background would no doubt be fair to the Muslims. The ambassador promised to do his best to help.

I really was quite anxious about the vote. I said to myself that if I lost, few people with my ethnic and religious background would be nominated in the future by the United States for such important positions.

The elections were held on Wednesday, 14 March. All but two of the candidates were present in the General Assembly hall. There was palpable tension in the air. The meeting started at 10 am and was suspended at 10.50 to count the paper ballots. As this was a secret ballot, electronic voting was not an option. At 12.35 the president of the General Assembly announced the results of the first ballot and the names of the twelve candidates elected. I was one of them. So for me the tension was over.

It took repeated ballots for the remaining two seats to be filled. Finally, by 8 pm the meeting rose with fourteen judges having been elected and all the fourteen vacancies filled. The Ukrainian candidate, Volodymyr Vasylenko, did not obtain the required majority, and so the Ukrainian request for additional time for the submission of candidates, to which I owed my nomination, did not help that country at all.

So there I was, having been elected. But was I truly ready? Clearly not. But I still had eight months before moving to The Hague. I was committed to giving a somewhat abbreviated seminar at NYU Law School in the autumn, but the rest of the time would be devoted to the study of criminal procedure,

IN THE US STATE DEPARTMENT

preparing for The Hague. Fate made me – a Holocaust survivor – a UN war crimes judge. Now it was up to me to be a good judge and dispense justice fairly.

10

FROM THE CHAIR TO THE BENCH

The modern enforcement of international humanitarian law started in Nuremberg. Yet, despite the normative influence of the Nuremberg proceedings, the international enforcement of atrocity crimes went nowhere until the creation by the UN Security Council of the International Criminal Tribunal for the former Yugoslavia (ICTY) in 1993 to try perpetrators of atrocities committed in the Balkans, followed in 1994 by the Rwandan tribunal (ICTR) and others, and eventually the International Criminal Court (ICC) in 1998. The establishment of the ICTY was made possible by the disintegration of the Soviet Union and the consequent attenuation of the longstanding paralysis in the Security Council. Rapidly, international impunity yielded, at least for a while, to a situation in which international criminal tribunals became an important part of the international community's response to genocide, crimes against humanity, and war crimes. I should add that the mandate of the ICTR included genocide and crimes against humanity but not war crimes, as the conflict in Rwanda was largely non-international.

A THOUSAND MIRACLES

Following my election as a judge of the ICTY by the UN General Assembly, I found myself starting a new career as an international criminal judge at the precocious age of seventy-one. For a person catapulted to an international criminal court after a quarter of a century of teaching, principally at the NYU School of Law, the change was momentous, even existential. I had got used to my habits as a professor, and they had guided me over so many years. Changing one's habits and, even more, one's instincts is always hard, and grows harder with age.

In many professions, a person can take time to gradually move into a new environment, place, habits, instincts. But a judge is not an intern; his is not a temporary, probationary appointment. He cannot just learn on the job. He must perform as a judge from the word go: he must hit the ground running. During my first few months as a judge, I do not know how I would have managed without my judicial clerks, to whom I will always be grateful.

Academic habits learned over the years – from obsessing over footnotes on abstruse questions to drawing analogies from across the length and breadth of the law – had rapidly to yield to a new way of thinking, requiring a laser-like focus on the immediate facts and the law of the case, from the general to the very concrete. And knowing that my work would have an immediate impact on the liberty or confinement of people made it so much more difficult.

I had to move from the luxury of contemplating theoretical questions and advancing ideas about the law to agonizing over the justice of acquitting or convicting a person charged with the gravest crimes known to humanity, and to heeding principles of judicial restraint and economy in my judicial writing. I had to forsake the comfort gained from circulating drafts to academic peers and learning from their comments, and follow instead a solitary decision-making process in which, save in deliberations, a hearing or a judicial opinion, one may share one's thoughts and concerns only with a few fellow judges and a law clerk or two, at best.

An academic typically engages in scholarly debates and enjoys responding to critics. Although judges have some limited latitude with regard to whether it would be appropriate for them to respond to criticism of their judicial decisions, many, perhaps most, including myself, choose not to do so. What could be more different from academic exchanges than the constant caution and frequent silence required of judges, who have to watch every word, gesture and ruling, not to reveal their thinking prematurely to the public, to the parties, sometimes even to colleagues. In other words, they must refrain from doing anything that might prejudice the appearance of impartiality and independence or risk the possibility of recusal or disqualification. These obligations are even more pronounced for the presiding judge, a position I occupied during much of my tenure on the court. In the deliberations of judges, I, as presiding judge, would speak last, so as not to be suspected of trying to influence my colleagues. Even when invited to give academic lectures, a judge must be careful when discussing past or present cases, or speculating aloud about future litigation. And while following all these *ex abundante cautela* rules, the presiding judge must know that their success, and the success of the court, may depend on their ability to lead – albeit cautiously, discreetly – to obtain or maintain consensus or, at least, a clear majority of the bench.

The life of a judge – in their work and even in their private comportment – is much more circumscribed by rules and traditions than the life of a teacher. Both national and international courts have typically adopted codes of professional and ethical conduct, which often include disciplinary rules to ensure compliance and accountability. Adopting disciplinary provisions is vital to demonstrate that judges take seriously adherence to the rule of law, and that everyone, including judges, must be subject to the enforcement of legal rules and principles designed to govern their conduct – in short they must be accountable.

One recurring matter concerns the involvement of judges in public debates. Here I note that convention advocates reticence and refraining from discussing individual cases. However, many aspects of the administration of justice and the functioning of the judiciary are the subject of legitimate public consideration and debate. In public debates there is the risk of different judges expressing conflicting views. Letting judgments speak for themselves is perhaps the safest solution.

My experience as an international criminal judge has been exhausting at times. It has been disquieting, frustrating and, practically always, solitary. It is painful to weather stoically, without responding, even the most hostile and offensive attacks and criticism. Yet, my years on the appeals bench or as a president (or chief justice) of the court have also been extraordinarily exciting and rewarding. There is absolutely nothing for which I would exchange them.

The kind of intellectual overhaul I experienced in joining the international judiciary may be common for many of those who become judges in national courts as well. And, indeed, there is much about being a judge of an international criminal court that is similar to the experience of serving in the criminal courts at national level. Like judges in national courts, an international criminal judge hears arguments, sifts evidence, rules on diverse motions, considers novel questions of law, drafts decisions and judgments, and deliberates on verdicts and sentences. Like their counterparts in domestic systems, international criminal judges must put the fairness of the proceedings at the centre of all they do and be guided by their commitment to judicial independence and impartiality, to the transparent and public nature of the judicial process, and to the importance of reasoned judicial decisions.

FROM THE CHAIR TO THE BENCH

In other respects, however, the mission and the work of an international criminal judge are unique and different. At the most basic level, the cases tried by an international criminal judge are unparalleled in evidentiary and geographic scope and involve alleged crimes almost never prosecuted on a national level, such as genocide. An international tribunal does not have the luxury of relying on detailed criminal codes supported by a gloss of interpretative precedent, but must rely instead on typically skeletal statutes. Hence, to satisfy the principle of legality, international criminal judges have to ground their rulings in customary international law, the identification of which – given customary law's often indeterminate nature – requires a judge to exercise both discretion and creativity, while resisting any possible drift toward progressive law-making.

An international criminal judge cannot take for granted that their fellow judges, the advocates who come before them or the public at large share a common understanding about how the law or legal procedures should be understood or, indeed, how a case should be managed. Judges trained in the common law and those trained in the civil law come from different legal and social traditions and cultures, and value legal precedents and their import differently. This difference may affect how judges approach each new proposed ruling. Procedural and evidentiary rules, moreover, have to be developed and wielded in ways that harmonize diverse national precedents, legal traditions and a variety of models. This is no small challenge.

Approaches to judicial precedents vary according to the education and legal culture of judges and staff. Those trained in the common law are typically interested in situating proposed decisions in the context of precedents, and they will usually make an effort to distinguish any case that does not follow such precedents. For legal certainty and fear of reversal, courts try to follow precedents as far as possible and appropriate. On the other hand, judges and staff trained in the civil law tend to follow past precedents as part of the jurisprudence but may be less systematic in canvassing them. They may be more inclined to anchor their decisions in a general theory of law. For all judges, the use of precedents, which prioritizes certainty in the law, has to be balanced against the interests of justice and the need to allow for the evolution of the law.

Academics often change their position on the law. For judges acknowledging error or otherwise departing from previous judicial positions, whether to promote a desirable evolution of the law or to comply with the requirements of justice, due process and the rule of law, the change is more difficult, as it may have implications for guilt, for innocence, for liberty or the deprivation of liberty.

Even though the accused who come before international criminal courts are always tried as individuals, the work of those courts and the fate of the individuals accused are often taken as emblematic of broader political considerations. More than anything else, it is this broader political and historical context in which international criminal judges work – the conditions in which the court was created, the sensitive and often horrifying nature of the allegations at stake, the rank or seniority of those who typically stand accused, the ongoing struggles among ethnic and national groups fighting for the legitimacy of their own historical narratives, the conflicting visions of rights and wrongs, and the competing claims of victimhood. These explain the unique nature of an international criminal judge's professional challenges.

For an academic, taking an unpopular position may have some unpleasant consequences. For a judge, however, going against the current or the common narrative of guilt may impact on their prospects for renomination or re-election, especially in cases involving senior military or civilian leadership. Despite many years on the bench, I learnt this, painfully, from my experience in reversing the conviction of the Croatian general Ante Gotovina (as I shall detail later). But to be faithful to the judicial oath, to be impartial and independent, such extraneous or political issues must be pushed outside the judicial agenda and calculus. Even if an extraneous agenda is in itself desirable, it should be beyond the judge's compass.

One of the major differences from academia is that an academic can and typically does take sides. Not so for a judge, who must be not only independent but impartial and must stay above the fray. Given this context, it is perhaps inevitable that international criminal courts and their judges will face criticism for particular rulings. Of course, the right to publicly express disagreement with a judicial decision is an integral part of a free society and a free press. Just as obviously, judges cannot cave in to pressure, nor be swayed in any way by public sentiment or criticism. Extrajudicial considerations must remain outside a judge's decisional ambit, even at the cost of not being re-elected to judicial posts in courts where such re-election is allowed under their statutes. Yet criticism can nonetheless have a corrosive effect on the credibility of a court.

Some criticism may come from those who bear the greatest hopes for international criminal justice and the greatest expectations from the judges entrusted with carrying it out. Indeed, international criminal judges must often perform their work at the intersection of a myriad of strongly held and sometimes incompatible expectations about what role an international criminal court should play.

But we must be careful to recall what is the core mandate of an international criminal tribunal: it is to try individuals within the governing legal framework and to determine whether – given the specific evidence presented and admitted by the court – the responsibility of an individual accused of international crimes has been established beyond reasonable doubt. The demands of due process, the substantive legal requirements, and the precise nature of the evidence necessarily constrain the court's findings in a way that a more free-ranging inquiry outside the judicial process – as in the case of truth commissions – would not. And, importantly, these same factors also permit different conclusions to be reached in different cases, meaning that responsibility for a crime may be found in one case while evidence of the same crime may be found insufficient in another.

Like everyone else, judges can and do make mistakes. I know I did, and at times I could have done things differently. But to be a judge, a person must at least try to live up to the lofty goals of the judiciary. They should try to ensure that the protections offered by the law are respected, equally, for the victims and for the alleged violators. They should remember that procedural fairness and due process are as important as substantive decisions, and that the core judicial norm is that convictions can only be entered or upheld on the basis of the evidence established beyond a reasonable doubt and in accordance with the law. They must at all times protect judicial independence and impartiality, avoiding not only bias but, just as importantly, the appearance of bias. It is only by respecting such principles that courts, especially international courts, can acquire credibility, authority and legitimacy.

Throughout my two decades on international criminal tribunals, I did my best to ensure the fairness of the judicial process.

Justice is not about achieving any particular outcome. It is about ensuring a principled process that serves to strengthen the rule of law and recognizes the overarching authority of the law. Not surprisingly, commitment to such principles to the exclusion of any extraneous agenda resulted at times in harsh, brutal and personal criticism of some of my decisions, especially

FROM THE CHAIR TO THE BENCH

those involving acquittals and early releases of prisoners from serving their prison sentences. These caused me much pain. But being a target of criticism should perhaps be regarded as part of the job description of an international criminal judge.

11

LIFE AT THE HAGUE

My election as a judge by the UN General Assembly in March 2001 was everything I wished for at the time. To be able to contribute to international justice was a dream come true. At the same time Monique was retiring from the UN and was happy to relocate to The Hague with me.

As I was to take up my functions as a judge on 17 November 2001 after being sworn in, we arrived a few days earlier at Amsterdam airport, where a car from the tribunal was waiting to take us to a hotel. We were excited but also anxious about starting our new life. Our first priority was to find a place to live. Our vision of our life in the Netherlands was more romantic than realistic, and we had dreams of settling on a canal or somewhere else with a nice view.

An invitation by my International Court of Justice colleague Dame Rosalyn Higgins led us to an eighteenth-century townhouse on a canal, with a Delft blue tiled kitchen and furnished with antiques, owned by a retired Dutch ambassador. The rent was on the high side, but we were not knowledgeable enough to bargain. We agreed to everything without any prior consideration of the practical issues. Soon we realized we had been too hasty. The windows were not well sealed and provided little protection from winter winds, and the central heating functioned poorly. We were constantly shivering in our quasi-palatial splendour. While Monique spent a lot of time lying in bed in the daytime, covered with blankets, I at least could keep warm in the tribunal building, which had housed an insurance company before.

Eventually, when my friend and chef de cabinet Larry Johnson left The Hague to return to New York, we took over his apartment in Hoge Nieuwstraat, where we had a much more modern, well-heated and better-equipped duplex. We missed the canal but were compensated with an unobstructed view of the old houses of parliament and the Mauritshuis museum.

Living in the city centre presented advantages; we could walk to most restaurants and shops, museums and cinemas, or hop on a tram. But on clear days, I much preferred going to work on foot. Strolling away from the city centre, I headed in the general direction of the sea, passed the magnificent Peace Palace, which hosts the principal judicial organ of the United Nations, and carried on through the Scheveningse Bosjes park before reaching the tribunal.

Monique had made a sacrifice in following me to The Hague as she was quite isolated at first. Although most Dutch speak English, Monique, who was shy, was quite lonely. But after I started my functions at the tribunal, she made friends with some of the judges' spouses. They too had accompanied their spouses and found themselves quite isolated even though they came and went, usually being in charge of families and properties back home. When they were in town, though, the spouses organized meetings and went on outings together to explore the country. Monique enjoyed their company.

Workwise, my joining the ICTY meant, first and foremost, submersion in the world of international justice and the bloody

LIFE AT THE HAGUE

history of the Balkans and of Rwanda. The kingdom of Yugoslavia had been created after World War I. After World War II, the Federal People's Republic of Yugoslavia was proclaimed in 1945, led by the Croat-born communist Josip Broz Tito, who ruled the country with an iron fist, suppressing ethnic and regional nationalism. Following his death in 1980, the federation fell apart and its constituent republics declared their independence. This triggered bloody wars as Croatia came to blows with Serbia, and Bosnia-Herzegovina with both Serbs and Croats. These conflicts were characterized by a plethora of crimes: at least one atrocity defined as genocide (Srebrenica) and thousands of crimes against humanity and war crimes. Mass rapes were committed by all parties (perhaps more by the Serbs) as a tool of ethnic cleansing, along with forced expulsion of people, killings, and the destruction of places of worship. Eventually, the principal armed conflict in Bosnia-Herzegovina between Bosniaks and Serbs, and between Bosniaks and Croats, was ended by the Dayton Agreement of 14 December 1995.

Meanwhile, in April 1994, Hutus in Rwanda committed large-scale killings of Tutsis, amounting to genocide. The killings eventually ended with the victory of a Tutsi army, under the leadership of Paul Kagame, who is still the president of the country. Crimes committed by the Tutsis have not been prosecuted because of the refusal of the Tutsi government.

These ethnically charged conflicts in the Balkans and in Rwanda sent shock waves throughout the world and were widely reported in all media, especially television, creating a strong pressure for accountability. At that time, there was a relaxation of tensions between the United States and Russia in the Security Council, enabling the establishment of the International Criminal Tribunal for the former Yugoslavia (ICTY) in 1993, with retroactive competence back to 1991 (the beginning of the Balkan wars), and the International Criminal Tribunal for

Rwanda (ICTR) in 1994, both under Chapter VII of the UN Charter, the only chapter of the UN Charter whose requirements are compulsory for member states. Both tribunals were fully funded by the regular budget of the United Nations, to which all member states are bound to make annual contributions.

The ICTY was given jurisdiction over the crime of genocide, crimes against humanity and war crimes. The ICTR, whose conflicts were considered as non-international, was given jurisdiction over genocide and crimes against humanity (as war crimes were still thought to involve only international armed conflicts). The jurisprudence and the achievements of these two tribunals paved the way for the establishment in Rome in 1998 of the International Criminal Court (ICC), the first and only permanent international criminal court.

At the NYU Law School, where I specialized in human rights and international humanitarian law, I had followed closely media reports of wide-scale crimes in the former Yugoslavia, and especially mass rapes. As a member of the Council on Foreign Relations in New York, an influential and powerful NGO, I was the rapporteur of a working group in 1993 advocating the creation of a tribunal for war crimes committed in Yugoslavia. This led me to write an article entitled "The Case for a War Crimes Tribunal for the Former Yugoslavia" for *Foreign Affairs* magazine.

Once I arrived in The Hague to take up my judgeship, I joined former national and international judges, prosecutors and professors who had been appointed to the ICTY. Judges were assigned to trials or appeals cases, and I was asked to join the appeals chambers. In February 2003, Judge Claude Jorda, who was then president of the ICTY, was elected to a judgeship in the ICC and stepped down from the ICTY before the end of his term. On 27 February I was elected to the presidency by consensus to cover the end of his mandate. In November I was

LIFE AT THE HAGUE

re-elected president for a full two-year term and then, after a pause, elected again in 2011 until 2013 and from 2013 to 2015. Overlapping with this, I was appointed (by the UN Secretary-General) president of the Residual Mechanism for International Criminal Tribunals in 2012 to deal with contempt of court and review cases, and was reappointed in that office until January 2019. For my last few years at The Hague, I therefore double-hatted as president of two institutions. I thus had the honour of leading the tribunals at The Hague for much of my tenure as a judge.

As president of the ICTY, I had to manage the institution, oversee the work of the registry, assign judges to chambers, supervise several trial chambers, preside over appeals benches and their deliberations, and represent the ICTY in the Security Council and the General Assembly. On every visit to the UNHQ I would meet the Secretary-General of the United Nations, the legal counsel and his deputy, and heads of administration and budget. I would also travel, from time to time, to the capitals of our client states and especially the permanent members of the UN Security Council, and plead for maximum support. In particular I often visited France, the United Kingdom and the United States. The year I had spent in UNITAR (United Nations Institute for Training and Research) as a Rockefeller Foundation fellow and my past work in the Israeli mission to the UN greatly facilitated my contacts with UN officials. And, of course, I frequently met with Dutch officials, as the tribunal relied heavily on the Dutch government for all kinds of assistance.

As president, I had to report orally to the Security Council every six months as well as to the working group on the tribunals, which consisted of all members of the Security Council and which was chaired by a non-permanent member. I first appeared before the Council on 23 November 2004 and made my last appearance on 11 December 2018, fourteen years later.

A THOUSAND MIRACLES

I still remember how awed I was on the first occasion. The procedure was that the president, on behalf of the Council, would invite the representatives of our client states – Bosnia, Croatia, Rwanda and Serbia – to participate in the meeting as well as myself and the prosecutor. The prosecutor and I would then take our seats at the Council table. The two of us would then report orally. These reports would be followed by presentations by members of the Council and finally by our client states.

To my surprise, I was able to make my presentations without showing how nervous I was. Even more surprisingly, there were some aspects of these appearances which I positively enjoyed. During my first years members would ask questions and I would be allowed to reply right away. My classroom experience of being obliged to think on my feet proved useful here. Unfortunately, over time the meetings became more formal and there was no chance of replying immediately; instead I included my responses in my next formal statement. However, in the Council's working group, most of the time was taken up by an active exchange of questions and answers, which I enjoyed greatly.

The missions to the UNHQ involved additional diplomatic activities. There was always a formal visit to the UN Secretary-General, with photographs taken, a handshake, a meeting across the table, a brief report from me, and some prepared comments from the Secretary-General. I was typically accompanied by my able chef de cabinet, Gabrielle McIntyre of Australia. During my presidencies I thus met and worked with several Secretary-Generals: Kofi Annan of Ghana, Ban Ki-moon of Korea and António Guterres of Portugal. Kofi Annan had a sparkling intelligence and instinctive warmth, and, from his earlier work as under-secretary-general for peace-keeping operations, he possessed excellent knowledge of the Balkans. Annan's successor, Ban Ki-moon, seemed well briefed though reserved. Guterres was truly interested and humane, projecting competence and serenity. When I resigned from the Residual Mechanism in November 2021, he sent me a warm letter of appreciation.

During Annan's tenure I had a major problem as many states were in arrears in making their annual contributions, and although the tribunal's budget was part of the general budget of the UN, the UN Secretariat ordered a hiring freeze in the ICTY (and the ICTR). Thanks to Annan's sympathetic understanding, the freeze was lifted after a few difficult months.

During my missions, I tried to meet the members of the Security Council and leading members of the General Assembly, to report, update, and mobilize support for the tribunal. It was difficult to get appointments with the heads of mission of the permanent members of the Council, so I would usually see either the deputy permanent representative (of the United States, the UK and France, typically) or the legal adviser. The UK mission seemed to be the best informed and most interested, and asked detailed and focused questions. Russia was always the most difficult and obstructive: it opposed the ICTY and the Mechanism, perhaps because of its close relationship with Serbia.

Then there were the special occasions, which I used for promoting support for international criminal justice. One such was my briefing of the Security Council under the Arria formula on 11 March 2019, which I gave after my presidency ended but still as a judge of the Mechanism. The formula was named after Diego Arria, president of the Council in 1992, when it was first used to invite speakers to address Council members in an informal meeting. This provided the possibility for exchanges between members of the Council and other stakeholders, such as civil society. In my briefing I spoke of the state of international criminal justice.

Finally I gave my swansong to the Security Council on 11 December 2018, when I stepped down as president of the Residual Mechanism. In the debate that followed, several members of the

A THOUSAND MIRACLES

Council made generous comments about my contributions to international criminal justice, among them Ambassador Karel van Oosterom of the Netherlands, the host country of the tribunals, who thanked me for leaving behind "an exemplary institution". My contribution to international criminal law, he said "has been truly extraordinary and indispensable to its development".

∞

The ICTY operated in the context of ongoing struggles among the former Yugoslavia's constituent countries and their ethnic, national and religious groups fighting for the legitimacy of their historical narratives, conflicting visions of rights and wrongs, and competing claims of victimhood. Trials and appeals often involved key military generals like the Bosnian Serb army's Ratko Mladić, Radislav Krstić, Zdravko Tolimir, Stanislav Galić and Ante Gotovina of Croatia; past presidents like Slobodan Milosević of Serbia (who died in detention) and Radovan Karadžić of Republica Srpska, a self-proclaimed Serb republic within Bosnia; and heads of security services. They were all considered heroes in their own countries. These cases were, of course, highly political.

Our trials were so much bigger than national criminal cases, much longer and more costly. I therefore appointed a committee to speed up our work. Cases not infrequently took several years, involving multiple crimes committed over long periods of time and in many localities. They necessitated travel by witnesses and translations of voluminous documents. We had to rent a wing of The Hague prison for our detainees.

As presiding judge of the Appeals Chambers for the ICTY and the ICTR, I sat on cases and participated in and chaired deliberations. Uncertainties in the law had to be considered and clarified. In the case of Galić we fleshed out rules pertaining to the conduct of hostilities, and in that of Dragoljub Kunarac, of which I am particularly proud, we reformed the rules on rape and torture. Over time I presided over nearly forty appeals, most of which ended with the confirmation of convictions, and a few in their reversal. Although I was highly criticized for the latter, my lodestar was always fairness and a sober, principled approach to process.

Presiding over the deliberations of judges to determine, by a simple majority vote, the outcome of an appeal was a critically important part of my duties, and one subject to the principle of secrecy in the judicial decision-making process. In deliberations, I always spoke last, not to unduly influence the process. As presiding judge of the two appeals chambers, I had to learn to combine fairness with firmness towards appellants, who often attempted to use the proceedings as pulpits for political statements or to obstruct the course of justice. The work never ended.

Luckily I could rely on the strong support of a very efficient staff in my cabinet and my legal team. I cannot mention all of them, but I am grateful to them for their assistance and friendship. Jonathan Cederbaum, Larry Johnson and Gabrielle McIntyre were, successively, my chefs de cabinet, and Alexi Zervos and Willow Crystal deputies. Jean Galbraith was a truly exceptional law clerk. Karen Johnson, head of my office in Arusha, Tanzania, was a particularly close collaborator.

My colleagues were friendly and I had the good fortune of having excellent legal clerks. Over time, approximately forty worked with me before going on to brilliant careers. They have remained good friends. I am truly grateful to all of them for helping me become an international criminal judge and making my experience so rewarding and interesting.

I used to tell every new law clerk that I expected an honest opinion from them. I put a premium on their challenging me on judicial matters, and discouraged flattery and pats on the back. This worked very well, as our relationship developed into something like a graduate seminar, in which questioning was encouraged, and it all produced good judicial decisions.

I was also very lucky with my driver. Najam Khan from Pakistan was well read, well informed and a great conversationalist. He had the perfect bearing of an English butler and reminded me a bit of the butler in *Downton Abbey*.

Despite the heavy workload, we were invited to a lot of receptions and cocktail parties by ambassadors and others. Once a year, Queen Beatrix and, later, her successor King Willem-Alexander would invite the entire diplomatic corps to a New Year's reception in the Dam, the royal palace in Amsterdam. This meant that Monique and I, and the other judges and their spouses, had to be driven to Amsterdam, early in the morning, often in heavy traffic. Though the palace glittered with its gilded furnishings, it had a certain austerity.

Those invited had to abide by a strict dress code and men had to wear a morning coat. The Queen or the King would give a short speech. The receptions in the Dam lasted for three hours or so, and protocol did not allow anyone to leave before the "royals". But the receptions provided an opportunity to meet the Sovereign and members of the royal family, and talk to colleagues and diplomats. If a member of the royal house wanted to have an individual conversation with a guest, the latter would be notified in advance, and would have to wait in a designated place for his or her turn.

I used one of these occasions, while talking to Queen Beatrix, to invite her to visit the ICTY. A few weeks later, her chef de cabinet informed me that she would like to co-chair a plenary of judges and asked me to prepare files on topics for possible discussion. Her visit on 5 October 2004 was a great success, as she spent three hours at the tribunal, in the plenary of judges and in a courtroom in which a trial was being conducted. I was immensely impressed by her mastery of the topics she had selected for discussion, her openness and her interest in staff members, and not only the senior ones.

I also had the privilege to talk several times with Princess Margriet, a sister of Queen Beatrix. She was very active in the Netherlands Red Cross and, as I was involved in various activities of the International Committee of the Red Cross myself, we had a common interest. On one occasion she asked me to review a lecture she was preparing, which I agreed to gladly. What impressed me was that when the paper was ready, her husband, Professor Pieter van Vollenhoven, a commoner, came to pick it up. I admired the modesty of the Dutch royal family.

As president of the ICTY, I had several interesting experiences with the Dutch civil service. One, in particular, in 2005 involved a senior staff member, a French magistrate, Catherine Marchi-Uhel, whose sick and paralysed mother needed full-time care while Catherine worked. Catherine had brought with her to the Netherlands a Kosovar couple who provided excellent care to the mother before the daughter joined the tribunal. One day, however, the Dutch authorities decided to order their deportation, as they did not have the necessary documents for residing in the Netherlands.

I felt that the enforcement of the deportation order would be a tragedy for Catherine, who could not continue working, and for the Kosovar couple, and appealed to the authorities. Not having much luck with lower-ranking civil servants, I approached the permanent secretary of the Ministry for Foreign Affairs, Mr F.A.M. Majoor, who, after considering the situation, reversed the deportation order and granted the Kosovar couple residence status. Eventually they obtained Dutch nationality. We became friends.

Otherwise, the Dutch were always correct, but although we lived in the country, we did not have much of a chance to socialize with many local people. The exceptions were my good friend Theo Van Boven, a prominent human rights scholar and activist who had been the first registrar of the ICTY; Judge Orie, with whom I shared a passion for music; and Nora Stehouwer-Van Iersel, the Dutch ambassador for international organizations, who, through our working exchanges, became a friend. My experience with the Dutch reminded me a bit of similar traits of the Swiss, who tended to keep to themselves.

The year 2003, my first as ICTY president, was particularly busy. On 23 May, I issued a public statement on the occasion of the anniversary of the tribunal's first decade. I noted that our collective labours had made a fundamental contribution to bringing justice to the people of the former Yugoslavia. Our trials had a broader significance as well, being the historic first step towards ending a tradition of impunity for mass crimes by establishing an effective system of international justice. But we recognized that without bringing to trial the highest-ranking indictees, Karadžić and Mladić, the principal accused for the genocide in Srebrenica, our mission would remain unfulfilled.

Over subsequent years I made many visits to individual Balkan countries, including Bosnia, Serbia and Montenegro, where I met with senior leaders and urged their cooperation with the work of the tribunal, especially by facilitating the arrest and transfer to the ICTY of those responsible for war crimes. For instance, on 10 November 2005 I made a working visit to Belgrade, meeting Prime Minister Vojislav Koštunica and other leaders. This was an important occasion, as I felt compelled to publicly criticize the Serbian government for non-cooperation in arresting the fugitives from the ICTY. In the press release I stated:

> I am of course aware that we have seen considerable progress in cooperation between the authorities here in Belgrade and the ICTY ... However, the international community is truly impatient about the endless delays in the fulfillment by Serbia of its remaining international

LIFE AT THE HAGUE

obligations. This is especially so regarding the failure to deliver Ratko Mladić.

This attracted a comment from the *New York Times* on 12 November:

> The United Nations war crimes tribunal stepped up its pressure on Serbia to deliver its top fugitives to the court by the end of this year. Failing to do so could jeopardize Serbia's ongoing talks for membership with NATO and the European Union, said Zoran Stanković, the Serbian defense minister. He said the warning came from the tribunal's president, Theodor Meron, who met with Serbian officials in Belgrade, including Mr Stanković. In a statement, Judge Meron said that the fugitives, who include Ratko Mladić and Radovan Karadžić, 'are within the reach' of the Serbian authorities.

In the private meeting I had with the prime minister I said also that Mladić and Karadžić would be making a mistake if they thought that they could wait out the term of the tribunal. Despite its completion strategy being in place, the tribunal would not close its doors until the two had been put on trial at The Hague. As with other accused, they were entitled to the full presumption of innocence. I also met other ministers, including the minister of defence, Zoran Stanković, a retired general, who did not give any signs of cooperation in securing Mladić. The meetings were truly difficult, with my Serb interlocutors avoiding making any clear commitments. But eventually all of the indicted persons were accounted for, which was a major success for our law enforcement.

In November 2018, I made another official visit to Belgrade. That visit reflected the tension between the ICTY and the government of Serbia. In my meetings with Serb leaders I reacted to Serbian denials of genocide in Srebrenica. A press release of 20

A THOUSAND MIRACLES

November described briefly my comments to Ana Brnabić, the Serbian prime minister:

> The President [Judge Meron] expressed disagreement and disappointment with the recent interview given by the Prime Minister in which she denied that the crimes committed in Srebrenica constituted genocide. He noted that numerous judgments before the International Criminal Tribunal for the former Yugoslavia made it absolutely clear that the crimes committed in Srebrenica in 1995 constituted genocide, including in the cases of Krstić and Tolimir, over which he presided. He further stated: 'It does not help the Government of Serbia to challenge judgments of a major international criminal tribunal.'

In concluding my account of my time at The Hague, I would like to tell the stories of two fellow judges with whom I was closely involved.

In 2004, our British judge, Richard May, was diagnosed with an aggressive brain cancer. He presided over one of the most important trials in the history of the tribunal, against the past president of Serbia Slobodan Milosević, who had been transferred to the custody of the ICTY on 29 June 2001. Judge May conducted the trial until 25 February 2004, when he had to step down because of his illness.

It was difficult to lose such a dedicated, brilliant colleague and a friend. But I had to quickly appoint Judge Robinson to replace May on the bench as, sadly, the rights of an accused do not allow for extensive breaks in trials, and judicial proceedings, like theatre shows, must go on.

On 22 February, the day of his resignation, I issued a statement describing his enormous contribution to international criminal justice. In it I cited a witness at the tribunal who described May as "made of reinforced platinum". Indeed, like platinum, May was strong, noble and of a very rare quality. Credible rumours circulated at the tribunal soon after my arrival that May was disappointed that a very experienced judge had been replaced by me, an academic without any courtroom experience. In his place, I would have felt the same. But it was a sign of his open mind and generosity that he became a close friend of mine and a valued mentor.

I knew that May's days were numbered. I also knew that the one thing that could make him and his wife Radmila at least a little happy was a knighthood, which he well deserved. I felt it was my duty to approach the British ambassador at The Hague. With incredible speed the UK government met the challenge. Judge May received a knighthood one week before his death on 1 July. I was happy that Sir Richard and Lady May could have some comfort in their darkest hours and that he secured the recognition he so amply deserved.

The other judge whom I wish to deal with here was Judge Aydin Sefa Akay of the Residual Mechanism, a national and resident of Turkey, who was arrested by the Turkish government in September 2016. Despite this causing serious problems with the proceedings in a Rwandan case which was being tried by a Trial Chamber panel of which Akay was a member, and despite the formal assertion of Akay's diplomatic immunity by the UN Office of Legal Affairs, on behalf of the Secretary-General, Turkey did not yield. I complained repeatedly of the violation of the rights of Judge Akay in every speech to the UN Security Council and the General Assembly, and raised the matter at every opportunity with the legal counsel of the UN and the Secretary-General, but to no avail.

On 14 June 2017, Judge Akay was convicted by a Turkish criminal court of membership of a terrorist group, FETO, and sentenced to imprisonment of more than seven years. In June 2018, all Mechanism judges were being considered for reappointment. Turkey objected to Akay's reappointment on the ground that as a convicted person, he no longer possessed the qualifications for appointment to the highest judicial office in Turkey, as required by the Statute of the Residual Mechanism. He was not reappointed by the UN Secretary-General. I reacted in a statement by expressing my disappointment and sadness, arguing: "judicial independence is a cornerstone of the rule of law, and it is longstanding and consistent practice to accord international Judges privileges and immunities in order to protect the independent discharge of their judicial functions".

On several occasions I raised my concerns with the media, including on CNN in Christiane Amanpour's programme on 7 December 2016.

> AMANPOUR: So what were the circumstances of the arrest of Judge Akay?
>
> MERON: He was arrested in September. And we in the United Nations, in the tribunal, in the office of legal affairs were given no notification of his arrest.
>
> AMANPOUR: Have you been able to talk to him? And do you have a satisfactory answer from the Turkish authorities as to why he's being detained and has he been charged with anything?
>
> MERON: Well, I don't have an answer in the technical sense, but I have been in touch with the son of the judge, who also happens to be his lawyer. And I understand that he has been charged with offences or attempts against the constitutional order of Turkey.
>
> AMANPOUR: And what is your reaction to that? Because, of course, their view is that he's been held because of some alleged conspiracy with the failed coup.
>
> MERON: Well, first of all, let me start by saying that everybody, judges included, enjoy a presumption of innocence. He's a very respected person. And I do fully respect the right of all states

LIFE AT THE HAGUE

to address their legitimate law enforcement concerns. That, of course, includes Turkey, but they must act according to due process and the rule of law.

AMANPOUR: What is your message to the Turkish authorities about Judge Akay?

MERON: Turkey has traditions stretching over centuries, during the Ottoman Empire. On the whole, they have the policy, highly supportive of privileges of minorities, that are open policy, protecting Christians, protecting Jews. In that great tradition, I would appeal to the government of Turkey, in a humanitarian spirit, to allow Judge Akay to be released from prison, to resume his functions as a judge of an international criminal tribunal. And by so doing, they will be not only demonstrating their interest in international justice, but also enabling us to fulfill a mandate given to us by the Security Council.

AMANPOUR: Let me ask you about the future of international criminal justice. Because you can see the pressure that the International Criminal Court is under with any number, right now, of African countries having pulled out and quite a lot of, you know, of assaults, verbal at least, on the court. For instance, from the Russian foreign ministry. "Unfortunately, the court has not justified the hopes attached to it and has not become a genuinely independent authoritative organ of international justice, revealing that in its 14 years of work," says the Russia foreign minister, "the ICC has pronounced just four verdicts and spent over $1 billion." Address those complaints.

MERON: Well, I think that all courts perhaps could find better ways of doing things. I think the ICC is a very complex institution. It is the only permanent International Criminal Court and thus it is the centrepiece of international criminal justice. I think that the recent withdrawals have been a blow, but as long as they do not become toxic, as long as they do

> not become viral, they can be contained. Indeed we have heard during the last few days that the Gambia may be withdrawing its abandonment of the court. But I think that with regard to international criminal justice, we really must go outside the box. And look more creatively at the whole issue. So we must have more international prosecutions. We must have more hybrid courts. Perhaps we should have more African or regional courts. Not at the expense of the ICC, but as a synergy with ICC. Serving a common holistic goal of advancing the cause of justice.

∞

Ending my presidency of the Residual Mechanism in January 2019 meant that the time had come to leave The Hague. My work there as a judge had been hard and difficult but rewarding. I felt good about my contribution to the development of international humanitarian law and accountability for war crimes. All the same, I was very sad to leave both my job and my staff. Still, I could look forward to continuing an active academic life in Oxford and doing some teaching at NYU. And, above all, I had Monique.

I felt too that my efforts had been recognized. On 20 June 2007 and 16 April 2014, in ceremonies at the French Embassy at The Hague, I was made an officer of the French Legion of Honour and was also given the "dignity" of Grand Officer of the French National Order of Merit for my being "one of the main actors of the emergence of international justice", according to the citation. On 16 May 2017, I was made an officer of the Polish Order of Merit. And on 15 January 2020, in the British Foreign Commonwealth and Development Office, I was invested with the title of Honorary Companion of the Most Distinguished Order of St Michael and St George (made substantive on 8 March

2022). Imagine, a scholar of chivalry being allowed to join a high order of chivalry!

> *Emiliya Viktorova, senior legal officer at the UN, speaking in Oxford in June 2024 on Theodor Meron's contribution to jurisprudence as a war crimes judge.*
>
> In essence, the international criminal tribunals have had the privilege of benefiting for two decades from Judge Meron's profound dedication to the principles of fairness, legality, impartiality, and humanity.
>
> It is, however, not only the quantitative aspects of the numbers of judgments, decisions or orders or the length of Judge Meron's service with the tribunals that I would like to highlight. Rather, it is Judge Meron's significant judicial contributions, for two decades, to the pursuit of justice for atrocity crimes. Two decades during which the Appeals Chamber, which Judge Meron presided over or of which he was a member of the bench, was called upon to provide authoritative interpretation of norms of international humanitarian law, international criminal law and international human rights law, setting important legal precedents for future criminal tribunals. To say the least, Judge Meron's judicial opinions shaped international criminal justice as we know it today …
>
> A central unifying theme of Judge Meron's jurisprudence at the ICTY, the ICTR and the Mechanism has been his unwavering commitment to ensuring that the protections afforded by the law are fully respected – whether these protections concern the victims of crimes committed in the context of an armed conflict or individuals who stand accused of such crimes …
>
> In his rulings on matters of substantive law, Judge Meron elucidated on numerous occasions key aspects that strengthened the protections afforded to civilians and other vulnerable individuals in time of armed conflict. As early as 2002, as a member of the bench of the Appeals Chamber in the *Kunarac*

et al. case, Judge Meron endorsed the trial chamber's definition of rape, rejecting the appellant's argument that the victim's continuing resistance should be an element of the offence as "wrong on the law and absurd on the facts". In the same case, Judge Meron and his fellow judges confirmed that the detention conditions in which a victim of sexual violence is being held could negate any possibility of consent. Judge Meron and his fellow judges also clarified that the public official requirement in the Convention Against Torture is not a requirement under customary international law in relation to the criminal responsibility of an individual for the crime of torture, outside the framework of the Convention ...

Judge Meron has also made key legal pronouncements in relation to the crime of genocide, which continue to resonate throughout the international community. In the *Krstić* appeal case, over which Judge Meron presided, the Appeals Chamber for the first time confirmed that genocide may be committed even in a small area or region and stated "unequivocally that the law condemns ... the deep and lasting injury inflicted and calls the massacre at Srebrenica by its proper name: genocide". Two years later, in the *Karemera et al.* case, the Appeals Chamber, with Judge Meron on the bench, held that "the fact of the Rwandan genocide is a part of world history, a fact as certain as any other, a classic instance of a 'fact of common knowledge'". The United Nations General Assembly has referenced both the *Krstić* appeal judgment and the *Karemera et al.* Appeals Chamber decision in its resolutions declaring 11 July as the International Day of Reflection and commemoration of the 1995 genocide in Srebrenica, and 7 April as the International Day of Reflection on the 1994 genocide against the Tutsi in Rwanda.

Still in relation to the crime of genocide, in the *Tolimir* case, over which Judge Meron presided, the Appeals Chamber clarified that threats of death and knowledge of impending death may constitute serious mental harm that amounts to an act of genocide, even if the victim survives. In the *Kalimanzira* case, likewise presided over by Judge Meron, the Appeals Chamber confirmed that direct and public incitement to commit genocide pertains to mass communications and may involve speeches made to large, fully public assemblies, as well as messages disseminated by the media.

Judge Meron's legal opinions have also clarified important aspects of the modes of liability applicable to international crimes. In the *Brđanin* case, the Appeals Chamber, presided over by Judge Meron, ascertained the contours of joint criminal enterprise liability in customary international law. In the interlocutory appeal in the case of *Hadžihasanović and Kubura*, over which Judge Meron also presided, the Appeals Chamber held that an accused charged with command responsibility may not be held responsible for crimes committed by a subordinate before the accused assumed command over that subordinate – a ruling rooted in Judge Meron's deep conviction of the need for criminal courts to abide by the fundamental principle of legality.

It is often emphasized that the success of a criminal tribunal is not measured by the number of acquittals or convictions. It is measured by its ability to deliver justice by ensuring the fundamental right of the accused to a fair trial. Ensuring respect for fair trial rights and due process protections has been central to Judge Meron's rulings throughout his judicial career …

In the *Nahimana et al.* appeal case, Judge Meron and his fellow judges determined that when an accused is represented, the presence of their counsel or co-counsel at hearings is essential and that evidence presented in their absence cannot be relied on against the accused. The vital importance of procedural justice is further exemplified by the decision in the *Zigiranyirazo* case, where the Appeals Chamber emphasized that the physical presence of an accused before the court is one of the most basic and common precepts of a fair criminal trial, and that testimony taken in the absence of the accused damages the integrity of the proceedings. In the same case, the Appeals Chamber, presided over by Judge Meron, reversed the accused's convictions, having found that the Trial Chamber misstated and misapplied the burden of proof with regard to the accused's alibi. In so doing, the Appeals Chamber underscored that the crimes the accused was charged with were very grave, thus meriting the most careful of analyses. This is yet another judicial decision that reflects Judge Meron's deep conviction that justice is not about achieving a particular verdict, but about a principled process and full compliance with the law and the evidence ...

Last but not least, a paramount consideration for Judge Meron throughout his service with the tribunals has been upholding the integrity of the judicial system. What better example in this respect than his decision, in response to the arrest of Judge Akay in Turkey, that judges of the Mechanism enjoy full diplomatic immunity, not only functional immunity, while performing their work, and that this full immunity is a cornerstone of an independent judiciary. In its recent judgment on application 59/17, the European Court of Human Rights cited Judge Meron's decision and arrived at the same conclusion in relation to the nature of Judge Akay's immunity.

The cited legal opinions are clear examples that, irrespective of the gravity of the charges, in his appellate jurisprudence Judge Meron never lost sight of the importance of ensuring that the judicial process is conducted with full respect for the fair trial rights of the accused, and in full compliance with the law and the evidence on the record.

And, above all, Judge Meron's principled positions, never compromising with the law irrespective of the parties to the conflict and at times strong political pressure, have always been and remain a true testament to his legal brilliance and judicial integrity.

LIFE AT THE HAGUE

Letter from US Secretary of State Antony Blinken, following my stepping down from the Residual Mechanism in November 2021.

THE SECRETARY OF STATE
WASHINGTON

December 28, 2021

The Honorable
Theodor Meron
Trinity College
Broad Street
Oxford, United Kingdom

Dear Judge Meron:

I am writing to thank you and to wish you well on your retirement as an international judge. Your exemplary service to the International Residual Mechanism for Criminal Tribunals, as well as your work as president of and appeals judge for the International Criminal Tribunals for the former Yugoslavia and for Rwanda has furthered justice, peace, and accountability for the worst kinds of crimes known to humanity. Your many years of distinguished contributions as a scholar, counselor of international law for the U.S. Department of State, and international judge have set a standard for integrity, fairness, and judicial independence. Having lived the horrors of the Holocaust, your lifework has built and implemented the tools to ensure, as Elie Wiesel once wrote, that "'Never again' becomes more than a slogan." You have made the world safer and more just. The United States is proud to have nominated you to the international bench.

On behalf of the entire Department of State and those many Department colleagues who have had the privilege of working with you over the decades, I extend our deepest thanks for your dedication and commitment to international justice. We wish you all the best in your ongoing scholarship at Oxford and hope your retirement from the bench brings additional opportunities to pursue your love of Shakespeare and theater.

Sincerely,

Antony Blinken

Antony J. Blinken

With gratitude and admiration for your extraordinary service to our country and to justice.

12

THE STATE OF INTERNATIONAL CRIMINAL JUSTICE

I am often asked a number of questions about international criminal justice. Do we really need international criminal tribunals? Is their object to serve the interests of the victims? Are international criminal courts successful? In this chapter I will try to share my thoughts on these three questions.

There are many possible answers to the first question, but I would single out one key point. The most obvious reason is that they provide a forum for dealing with high-level war criminals. Without international criminal courts, what would we do with alleged war criminals who have been captured? Letting them go free is untenable, as is summary execution or perpetual detention without trial. That leaves some form of legal process. But while trials in the countries of the accused or in the countries in which they committed the crimes may prove successful, on occasion – as with the trials of Germans accused in Leipzig following World War I – they have proved excessively lenient. In other cases, a government may harbour too much vengeance towards the accused, even the worst of the worst.

∞

I turn to the second question: do international criminal tribunals provide justice for victims?

As a victim of the Holocaust – or genocide, in today's criminal law terminology – should I have supported the view of those who, in the conflict between the various stakeholders of international criminal justice, give a clear preference for the interests of the victims? In making my choice, despite my experiences, I always chose the blindfolded goddess of justice. As a judge, it was my duty to decide by the law and by the evidence before me and dispense an impartial justice for all. Let me make it clear, however, that my refusal to prefer any group, even the victims, applies to criminal justice, not to other strategies essential for dispensing justice, as, for example, creating funds designed specifically to compensate victims, as Germany did so effectively in compensating the victims of the Holocaust.

One of the most frequently voiced expectations is that international criminal courts should give victims justice and facilitate closure. The idea that international criminal justice is done for the sake of victims is popular, just as it is contested. It risks pitting the aim of many victims of ensuring punishment of, and retribution against, those whom they believe to have committed crimes, on the one hand, against the rule-of-law guarantees of fairness, impartiality and due process, on the other. If one of the individuals accused of atrocities, and particularly one who is a political or military leader, is acquitted, or if the prosecution declines to pursue charges, these decisions are sometimes viewed as a failure of international criminal justice. So the legitimacy of acquittals is often called into question, and the virtue of convictions is extolled by the victims and their associations, often supported by

THE STATE OF INTERNATIONAL CRIMINAL JUSTICE

interested governments. But victims typically do not belong only to one party. Each party has its victims asking for justice.

Members of the public, including victims, often equate the bringing of heads of state, leaders of political parties, and leaders of military or paramilitary groups "to justice" with the entering of convictions. Accused who come before international criminal courts thus often come – in the public mind – with an existing narrative of guilt.

Acquittals and, often, early releases of prisoners in any system cause some level of controversy, and they unquestionably bring victims of crimes real pain. This controversy can be magnified at the international level, given the dimensions of the crimes alleged and the political implications of those allegations. Indeed, for victims, an acquittal may feel like a denial of what happened to them and a betrayal of their hopes and expectations. For others, an acquittal may be seen as a rewriting of history or a failure of the international court to serve its purpose as part of a broader agenda of transitional justice.

Take the unanimous reversal of the conviction for genocide and sentence of twenty years' imprisonment of Protais Zigiranyirazo on 16 November 2009 by the International Criminal Tribunal for Rwanda (ICTR) Appeals Chamber, over which I presided. The Rwandan minister of justice, Tharcisse Karugarama, reacted to the decision by saying that "it was a sad day for Rwanda, it is a sad day for genocide survivors". Often the reactions of Rwandan officials to acquittals or early releases were less polite.

I will always remember the delivery of that decision in our courtroom in Arusha. In the middle of my reading the summary of our judgment I heard someone sobbing. Soon I realized that it was the appellant's lawyer, John Philpot, who, I was told later, was so convinced of his client's innocence and so emotionally involved in the case that he started crying the moment he understood the appellant would be acquitted.

A THOUSAND MIRACLES

Out of thirty-one appeals from thirty-seven appellants (not counting review cases) from the ICTY, ICTR and the Residual Mechanism over which I presided, the convictions of eight prisoners were reversed, a number which is certainly not excessive (every fifth prisoner). I was always faithful to the basic judicial norm that a judge cannot follow any extraneous agenda, any purpose outside the narrow judicial issues before him, however desirable such a purpose may appear and whatever pressure may be applied by the media, governments or victims' organizations.

In my view, there would be a true failure of international criminal justice if international courts were to convict an individual on an inadequate evidentiary or legal basis. When the law or the evidence does not support a finding that a person is guilty beyond a reasonable doubt of the specific crimes for which he or she has been charged, it is the duty of international judges – it was my duty – to rule accordingly. In so doing, judges are not declaring an individual innocent, they are not redefining history, and they are not thinking about the impact on national or transnational reconciliation. They are – or, rather, we were – carrying out a responsibility to follow the dictates of the law, no more and no less.

For me, as a judge, bringing someone to justice meant simply that the individual charged should be tried fairly, soberly, in accordance with the law and the evidence, and after the court had heard from the parties and observed the time-honoured principles of fairness and the presumption of innocence. This is what the rule of law required on a domestic level and what it required no less on the international level.

Even as we sympathize with the sentiments of victims, the overarching obligation of a criminal judge – whether at the national or the international level – is to respect the fundamental principles of the rule of law, a concept still more fragile in international than in most domestic jurisdictions. It is through

THE STATE OF INTERNATIONAL CRIMINAL JUSTICE

affirming the importance of courts and due process – not simply in times of peace but in war and conflict and their aftermath – that we ensure that it is the law, and not the rifle or vengeance, that rules. This, to my mind, is the animating principle at the very heart of international justice, and the principle that has been at the centre of my work for two decades as an international criminal judge.

International criminal judges must often carry out their work at the intersection of a number of strongly held and sometimes incompatible expectations about what role an international criminal court should play. Preferring the victims is not the only expectation. Some stakeholders, for instance, look to international criminal courts to establish the "truth" of a particular horrific event or to create a definitive historical record. When the court's judgment fails to agree with an expected narrative of guilt or to find that a specific crime attributed to a particular individual has been committed by him or her, the claim is made that the court itself or the judges involved have failed in their mission.

There is no doubt that the quantum of evidence collected in relation to a case is often immense and a judgment memorializing such evidence can offer a detailed record of particular events. Moreover, for jurists coming from the civil law tradition with their investigating magistrates, truth-seeking may be seen as an essential component of international criminal justice, more so perhaps than in the common law with its adversarial system.

But we must be careful to recall what is the core mandate of an international criminal court: it is to try individuals within a governing legal framework and to determine whether – given the specific evidence presented and admitted by the court – the responsibility of an individual accused of international crimes has been established beyond reasonable doubt. The demands of due process, the substantive legal requirements, and the precise nature of the evidence necessarily constrain the court's findings in a way that a more free-ranging inquiry outside the judicial process would not. And, importantly, these same factors also permit different conclusions to be reached in different cases, meaning that responsibility for a crime may be found beyond reasonable doubt in one case while evidence of the same crime may be found insufficient in another.

In any event, international criminal tribunals have recognized the importance of creating a historical record by requiring the accused to state and acknowledge the facts in cases where guilty pleas have brought an end to a trial.

Other stakeholders may look to international criminal courts to bring about peace and post-conflict reconciliation, as indeed the UN Security Council and other bodies have at times suggested in establishing such courts. For those who believe that international criminal courts are mandated to promote peace and reconciliation, international criminal justice will almost invariably be found wanting where there is no evidence of any such impact or where rulings are thought to be counterproductive to reconciliatory aims.

Reconciliation is, of course, immensely important, going beyond any particular judicial decision. International justice can reach only a handful of perpetrators, while atrocities are typically committed by large groups. There can hardly be reconciliation between warring ethnic or religious groups without some acknowledgment of culpability, as in Germany following the Holocaust. And in many cases, each of the groups involved considers itself to be the victim.

As a judge, a president and presiding judge of appeals chambers, I have been severely criticized for reversing, in a few cases, convictions entered into by trial chambers. And I have been criticized by the Rwandan media for granting in many cases early release for prisoners who had served a substantial portion of their prison sentences and were thus eligible under our practice

THE STATE OF INTERNATIONAL CRIMINAL JUSTICE

for consideration for early release, which is within the discretion of the president. I found the criticism painful and believed that pressure exerted on presidents was dangerous to the principle of judicial independence.

One of the major difficulties with the present system of international criminal justice lies in its selectivity. This problem is not one for which judges bear responsibility. It is the states and international organizations such as the United Nations that establish, ratify and enforce the jurisdiction of international criminal tribunals. The Security Council has a major role to play in this regard, as it has the power to create ad hoc tribunals or to refer cases to the International Criminal Court (ICC). Recently either option has been cancelled by the use or threat of a veto by Russia, sometimes China, sometimes the United States.

The selectivity of international justice (which situations or cases become the focus of accountability efforts, and which do not) may be inevitable in many respects owing to both the limited jurisdictions and resources of international courts and the differing capacities of various national jurisdictions. Scarcity of resources means that international criminal tribunals are unable to take on all or even most of the cases that fall within their jurisdiction, and resource constraints may undermine the will to create new courts or jurisdictions. Practically speaking, it is simply not possible for international courts to try all of those accused of responsibility for international crimes. In sum, hard choices must be made.

At the same time, selectivity may also arise in a particularly nefarious manner when it is the result of political manoeuvring or alliances, such as when permanent members of the Security Council protect themselves, their own or close allies. Such selectivity is anathema to the rule of law (which requires equality in enforcement and non-arbitrariness), and has eroded support for and cooperation with international judicial institutions.

A THOUSAND MIRACLES

International criminal justice clashes with the phenomenon of selectivity. The simple fact is that, as I write, atrocities or war crimes are being committed in many countries without proceedings before the ICC in response to most situations, nor has there been any concerted effort on the part of the international community to establish specialized international tribunals to address them (although the UN General Assembly has established mechanisms for the collection and preservation of evidence for crimes committed in Syria, Iraq and Myanmar). Many arrest warrants of the ICC have not been executed, and the docket of the ICC has been modest compared with that of the UN tribunals. The selectivity reflected in the assertion of international criminal jurisdiction for some situations, and not for others, poses an enormous challenge not just for efforts to end impunity but for international justice itself and the rule of law.

Selectivity is, regrettably, in many ways a political and practical reality. Criminal tribunals at the supranational level are necessarily courts of limited jurisdiction – jurisdiction that may be exercised only over situations in states that have acceded to such jurisdiction or by the mandate of the Security Council under Chapter VII of the UN Charter. That limitation subjects the administration of international criminal justice to the vagaries and vicissitudes of politics, as a result of which some will prioritize alliances and self-interest over the rule of law. The tribunals and those who would wish to see international criminal jurisdiction asserted over new atrocities are often powerless in the absence of some form of national will or international political consensus. Indeed, the enforcement of international law depends on the political will of states.

Another aspect of selectivity is simply giving preference to prosecuting people who perpetrate crimes against group A, but not those who perpetrate crimes against group B. This is more of

THE STATE OF INTERNATIONAL CRIMINAL JUSTICE

a political than a legal problem. But it is also a problem for the credibility of the international justice system as a whole.

In some situations, most of the crimes are committed by one party, which is regarded in the public opinion as the principal perpetrator, while the other party tends to be regarded as the victim. But crimes, even those less egregious or less frequent, are committed also by those commonly considered victims. In the former Yugoslavia more crimes may have been committed by Serbs, but crimes were also committed by Croats and Bosniaks. The ICTY deserves credit for prosecuting crimes committed by all sides.

In the Ukraine war most crimes appear to have been committed by Russians. But some crimes may have been committed by Ukrainians as well. The ICC prosecutor is compelled to investigate and prosecute crimes committed by all or any parties, granted that they should be of sufficient gravity. In the context of the Ukraine war, he issued arrest warrants against President Putin and the Russian commissioner for violations of children's rights Mrs Lvova-Belova. But it remains to be seen whether efforts to prosecute Ukrainians would produce the necessary cooperation of Ukrainian authorities, or negatively impact on the overall cooperation of Ukraine in the collection of evidence on Russian crimes. The ICC prosecutor also issued arrest warrants against leaders of Hamas for crimes committed on 7 October 2023 and against two members of the Israeli cabinet for crimes committed in Gaza.

In Rwanda, crimes allegedly committed by the Rwandan Patriotic Front (RPF) were investigated by Human Rights Watch and other NGOs and, initially secretly, by Prosecutor Carla Del Ponte. Rwanda reacted to investigations by Del Ponte by making it impossible for witnesses to travel to the ICTR courthouse in Arusha, thus causing lengthy suspensions of trials. Of course, the immensity of the genocide committed by Hutus against

Tutsis and those who collaborated with Tutsis made the crimes allegedly committed by the RPF seem relatively minor, and made it politically difficult for those interested to insist on their serious investigation.

Eventually, the obstructions imposed by Rwanda paid off. Security Council Resolution 1503 of 28 August 2003, which dealt largely with the completion strategy of the ICTY and the ICTR, called on Rwanda and other states to intensify cooperation with the ICTR, "including investigations of the Rwandan Patriotic Front", but created the post of a separate prosecutor for Rwanda. By Resolution 1504 of 4 September 2003, Carla Del Ponte, until then prosecutor for both the ICTY and the ICTR, was appointed prosecutor of the ICTY only. The appointments were made by Secretary-General Koffi Annan with the consent of the Security Council. By Security Council Resolution 1505, also of 4 September, Hassan Bubacar Jallow of the Gambia was appointed prosecutor for the ICTR. I am not aware of any subsequent attempts to prosecute any members of the RPF. I recognize that Prosecutor Jallow reported to the Security Council that his office was continuing investigations of the RPF, and that decisions on whether to indict were based only on the evidence and the law.[1] But this did not result in a single indictment issued by Prosecutor Jallow. That was the end, as far as I know, of the ICTR's investigations of the RPF's alleged crimes. The outcome is not very reassuring for the rule-of-law principle of equal enforcement.

The question of equal justice for all arises not only with regard to who should be investigated or prosecuted but also with regard to the fairness of the practice of granting early release. In deciding early release applications, I was required as president,

---

[1] https://reliefweb.int/report/rwanda/rwanda-letter-hassan-b-jallow-kenneth-roth-22-jun-2009

THE STATE OF INTERNATIONAL CRIMINAL JUSTICE

under Rule 151 of the Rules of Procedure of the Mechanism, to consider the treatment of similarly situated prisoners as a factor. In an application I decided on 11 December 2012, an ICTR prisoner submitted that this factor should include consideration of the treatment of prisoners convicted by both the ICTR and the ICTY. Accordingly, based on the practice of the ICTY, the applicant submitted that, having served two-thirds of his sentence, he should be considered eligible for early release. He contended that serving two-thirds of the sentence was an appropriate eligibility threshold for the Mechanism to apply, in the light of established national and international practice.

The question before me was thus whether, for purposes of early release determinations under Rule 151, persons convicted and sentenced by the ICTR should be considered "similarly situated" not only to persons convicted and sentenced by the ICTR, but also to those convicted and sentenced by the ICTY or the Residual Mechanism. I was of the view that all prisoner populations to be ultimately supervised by the Mechanism should be treated equally. There was no compelling reason why convicted persons whose sentences were or will ultimately be supervised by the Mechanism should be treated differently for early release purposes depending on which tribunal convicted or sentenced them. The Mechanism is a single institution that succeeded both the ICTY and the ICTR (with one branch for each of those tribunals). I therefore considered it fair and just to deem early release applicants "similarly situated" to all prisoners whose sentences would be supervised by the Mechanism, irrespective of whether they were convicted or sentenced by the ICTR, the ICTY or the Mechanism itself.

Rwanda was, however, opposed to granting any early release and conducted a vigorous campaign against me through the media close to the government. It also put pressure on the United Nations with the object of trying to compel me to yield to its position. Faithful to my obligation as a judge and a president to uphold the independence of the international judiciary and convinced of the justness of the practice I followed, I did not yield. I appreciated the fact that the UN Secretariat never tried to persuade me to accommodate Rwanda.

In looking up recent practice on early release, I note that from the time I left the presidency of the Mechanism on 17 January 2019, until 2024, twenty-eight public decisions on early release were issued, about half of which concerned ICTR prisoners, but these did not include a single decision granting an early release to an ICTR prisoner. Of course, there may have been good reasons for all of the decisions denying early release. Judges may hold divergent views on the practice to follow. Another factor to consider is the different views of the states of the former Yugoslavia and of Rwanda. One may wonder, however, whether the government of Rwanda considers that its policy of pressure produced the intended results and was successful.

In fine, my lodestar for international criminal justice has always been fairness, justice, the principle of legality, due process, and the rule of law, on which the legitimacy of our project rests. I have not always succeeded. But at all times I did my utmost to uphold and protect the integrity of international criminal justice.

∞

I now turn to the third question: how well is international criminal justice doing? Here I will first address the challenges and then the achievements.

International criminal tribunals are unique in the sense that they are stand-alone courts, not supported by the apparatus of the state and, in contrast to Nuremberg, have no police powers or other enforcement capability. They depend on the cooperation of states for enforcement and resources. In the early years of the ICTY, the cooperation of states in arresting indicted persons and

THE STATE OF INTERNATIONAL CRIMINAL JUSTICE

in executing subpoenas was clearly unsatisfactory. Eventually, however, because of pressure by the European Union, United States and United Kingdom, and with help from Western intelligence services, all the 161 ICTY indictees were accounted for – a success of law enforcement by any standard.

In contrast to the ICC, the tribunals did not have an assembly of state parties to call upon, and had to assume a quasi-legislative role in adopting rules of procedure and evidence. This was a difficult but, in the end, successful process. There was a need to develop a constructive synergy between the common law adversarial system and the civil law inquisitorial system, and thus the diverse legal cultures of the judges. While the system started almost exclusively from the common law – and on the substance of the law it largely remained so – on major aspects of evidence it turned to the civil law. It thus dropped the hearsay rule, increasingly allowed written evidence, and enlarged the power of the judges to manage the conduct of proceedings. These changes have made the proceedings somewhat shorter and more efficient.

The length and the cost of the trials have been continuing challenges. Each case before an international criminal tribunal takes enormous time and resources. International criminal trials are usually long ones. Typically, they involve multiple crimes, committed over long periods of time and in many localities. They involve travel by witnesses and translations of voluminous documents. Because of difficulties in collection, evidence is often discovered late in proceedings. The tribunals had to develop procedures for introducing evidence even on appeal.

There are whole areas of the world that remain outside the jurisdiction of any international criminal tribunal. In these countries, which account for most of the world's population, and which are not party to the ICC, no international court has jurisdiction over crimes committed by citizens of these countries on their soil or elsewhere. The difficulties in apprehension often mean that trials occur years after the atrocities took place, if at all. The Cambodia tribunal deals with crimes that stem from the Khmer Rouge. Few of the witnesses are still around. Most of the genocidaires have died in the meantime, with impunity.

National jurisdictions seldom take advantage of the principle of universality of jurisdiction to prosecute alleged war criminals before their courts. The lofty principle of complementarity in the ICC Statute, which provides for the priority of the state in prosecuting war criminals in their custody, is seldom enforced. Moreover, many states that are party to the ICC Statute have not internalized the provisions of the Statute in their domestic legislation.

I turn now to the achievements of the international criminal courts.

These courts have developed international criminal law and international humanitarian law, some aspects of which were still skeletal at Nuremberg. They have succeeded in giving a fair trial to the suspected perpetrators of international crimes. In this respect they have greatly improved upon the protections available at Nuremberg. They have also elaborated norms in respect of war crimes, crimes against humanity, and genocide. They have established a corpus of rulings on procedure and evidence.

They have enhanced principles of fairness and legality and brought about a revival of humanitarian customary law. They have transformed norms originally established to govern the responsibility of states into norms specific enough to govern the criminal liability of individuals. They have ruled that most protective norms governing international armed conflicts apply also to non-international armed conflicts. They have triggered a rise (though still inadequate) in national prosecutions of atrocity crimes. In terms of due process, as well as substantive humanitarian and criminal law, modern international courts and tribunals are light years ahead of the proceedings at Nuremberg. To give one

THE STATE OF INTERNATIONAL CRIMINAL JUSTICE

example, there were three acquittals at Nuremberg – but I should add that there was no provision protecting acquitted individuals from being tried again for the same crimes. These acquitted men were seized and tried again by a German court. This cannot happen today. The guarantees now accorded to defendants in the foundational statutes of international criminal tribunals and in the case law are substantial, and the transparency with which international tribunals act provides a further safeguard.

On the positive side of the ledger, we have also succeeded in bringing a substantial number of high-level suspects from the former Yugoslavia and Rwanda to justice, and a small number of high-level suspects from African countries before the ICC. The experiences of the ICTY and ICTR have shown that where the international community provides sufficient resources and political support for tribunals, and where the European Union, the United States, the United Nations and NGOs encourage or pressure recalcitrant but susceptible states to hand over suspects, then we achieve results.

For another thing, we do have some domestic prosecution for international crimes, whether assumed voluntarily or under pressure from the international community. Given the limited capacity of international criminal courts, it is reassuring that there is a small but significant trend for individual states to enforce international law by holding accountable those who serve as accomplices to regimes that commit atrocities.

The most singular achievement of the ICTY and the ICTR has been their focus on and success in prosecuting and elaborating the crime of rape. This is in stark contrast with the Nuremberg and Tokyo trials. In the ICTY alone, 80 individuals, or almost half the 161 accused, had charges of sexual violence included in their indictments, and 36 were convicted for such crimes.

Does international criminal justice deter the commission of international crimes? Unfortunately, there is very little hard evidence on this front. We do have a plethora of sweeping statements, anecdotes and surmises. I note, for instance, that the 1995 genocide in Srebrenica occurred two years after the establishment of the ICTY. Perhaps the fear of prosecutions is a bit more real now, as I would like to hope, but only the future will tell. The possibility of international prosecutions should, however, be considered as only one possible tool of deterrence. Additional tools include targeted sanctions, seizure of assets, restrictions on travel, warrants of arrest, national prosecutions, and the exercise of universal jurisdiction in third states. I expect that arrest warrants issued by competent international jurisdictions, and particularly by the ICC, will be a major factor in deterrence. So will fear of arrest by a third country of an individual against whom an arrest warrant is pending.

Once again, it is difficult to measure whether, and to what extent, international criminal tribunals have in fact had a positive influence on the establishment of regional peace. We can try to draw some conclusions on this front from the experiences of the ICTY, the ICTR and the ICC to date. At the most basic level, these tribunals can contribute to regional peace by providing an internationally reputable mechanism for the removal of abusive leaders. The removal, for instance, of Radovan Karadžić from power and his indictment were essential for the implementation of the Dayton Agreements. The indictment of Charles Taylor, president of Liberia, had a similarly positive effect. But there is a flipside to this point, which is that peace may also become more difficult to achieve if leaders know that they will face international criminal prosecutions once hostilities are over.

A common claim is that in the course of holding wrongdoers accountable, international criminal tribunals break the cycle of vengeance and allow people to start moving forward. What is more, the very existence of international criminal jurisdictions introduces the paradigm of resolving conflicts by resorting to

THE STATE OF INTERNATIONAL CRIMINAL JUSTICE

justice, due process and law rather than to pogroms and vendettas. I support this argument both in the short term and in the longer term as part of educational and cultural changes.

The sanctions regime imposed on the ICC prosecutor in February 2025 is a major retrogressive step, which will inevitably promote impunity and make it much harder for the ICC to perform its mission. Depending on how it will be enforced and how long it will last, it may put the very existence of the ICC in real danger.

Despite the current retraction of international criminal tribunals, I recognize the great importance of the increased commitment of the international community to international criminal justice. International criminal tribunals have demonstrated that international prosecution and trial are both feasible and credible. To my mind there is no question that we must do our utmost to find ways to encourage states to prosecute war crimes before national judiciaries in accordance with international legal norms. This is not simply a question of numbers and practicality; this is an imperative if the new era of accountability is to truly take hold both globally and locally. We must continue to work to give renewed vitality to the principle of accountability, both internationally and domestically. And our lodestar must always be fairness and justice, principles on which the legitimacy of our project rests.

13

COMMEMORATING SREBRENICA AND REFLECTING ON GENOCIDE

As president of the ICTY and the presiding judge in the Krstić appeal judgment concerning the first genocide committed on European soil since World War II, I took part in several commemorations of the genocide in Srebrenica. On 11 July 2015 I was thus present at the service held at the cemetery of Potočari, close to the place where seven or eight thousand Bosnian men and boys of Srebrenica had been massacred by members of the Bosnian Serb Army under General Ratko Mladić twenty years earlier.

The podium was at the bottom of a sort of crater with sloping hills rising high above. Hundreds, perhaps thousands, of Muslim women in their traditional attire were sitting on the ground. I stood amid a sea of white gravestones, green coffins and sombre faces. In memory of those lost not far from there, I read aloud a passage from an appeal judgment in *Prosecutor v. Krstić*, the first appeal judgment to judicially recognize crimes committed at Srebrenica in 1995 as genocide. In doing so, the judgment not only acknowledged the crimes committed in Srebrenica for what they were, but also clarified the legal requirements of the crime of genocide, thereby facilitating the recognition and, hopefully, the prevention of the crime. On this occasion, I recognized, more than before, the power of the word "genocide". As I said:

> Among the grievous crimes this Tribunal has the duty to punish, the crime of genocide is singled out for special condemnation and opprobrium. The crime is horrific in its scope; its perpetrators identify entire human groups for extinction. Those who devise and implement genocide seek to deprive humanity of the manifold richness its nationalities, races, ethnicities, and religions provide. This is a crime against all of humankind, its harm being felt not only by the group targeted for destruction but by all of humanity.
>
> The gravity of genocide is reflected in the stringent requirements which must be satisfied before this conviction is imposed ... Where these requirements are satisfied, however, the law must not shy away from referring to the crime committed by its proper name.
>
> By seeking to eliminate a part of the Bosnian Muslims, the Bosnian Serb forces committed genocide. They targeted the extinction of the forty thousand Bosnian Muslims living in Srebrenica, a group that was emblematic of the Bosnian Muslims in general. They stripped all the male Muslim prisoners, military and civilian, elderly and young, of their personal belongings and identification, and deliberately and methodically killed them solely on the basis of their identity. The Bosnian Serb forces were aware, when they embarked on this genocidal venture, that the harm they caused would continue to plague the Bosnian Muslims.
>
> The Appeals Chamber states unequivocally that the law condemns, in appropriate terms, the deep and lasting injury inflicted, and calls the massacre at Srebrenica by its proper name: genocide. Those responsible will bear this stigma, and it will serve as a warning to those who may in future contemplate the commission of such a heinous act.[1]

---

[1] *Prosecutor v. Radislav Krstić*, Case no. IT-98-33-A, Judgment, 19 April 2004, paras 36–37 (alterations in paragraph breaks added), www.unmict.org

COMMEMORATING SREBRENICA

Suddenly I heard tremendous applause. I had no idea why. Only after the ceremony did I hear the explanation. From the many speakers in the commemoration, I was the first speaker who had called the massacres by their proper name: genocide. I continued:

> But while it is vital that those who are believed to be responsible for committing crimes such as genocide be called to account through fair court proceedings, we must remember this: the judgments of a court alone cannot heal the deep wounds inflicted by crimes such as those at Srebrenica. Court rulings on their own cannot bring about reconciliation – and they cannot bring back those who were lost. For those of us who have seen so many of our loved ones perish – whether during the Holocaust or at Srebrenica – we know this all too well.
>
> Instead, it often falls to members of the communities most impacted by a crime – to civic and religious leaders, to parents and teachers, and to individuals like the Mothers of Srebrenica and members of other victims' groups – to find the strength and the means to rebuild their communities. Whatever else we have achieved in international justice, it is clear that Srebrenica will not be forgotten.

Some years later, I reiterated these points in London, at Lancaster House, during the Srebrenica memorial week.

> The judgment in the Krstić case was just one of scores of judgments rendered by the ICTY, each of them addressing extraordinarily complex cases involving allegations of the very worst crimes imaginable – and each of them, in different ways, a testimony to the condemnation expressed by international law and the international community for the heinous crimes that were the subject matter of the proceedings of the ICTY and the ICTR. I am proud of all that the Tribunal has achieved since it was established in 1993, and of its contributions to the creation of a new world in which ensuring accountability for crimes is increasingly the expectation – rather than the exception.
>
> To be sure, the judgments of courts can contribute in a meaningful way to a broader understanding about a conflict. They can help to

restore respect for the rule of law, and can – as the Krstić judgment did – offer some solace to survivors by recognizing a crime for what it is.

It falls to members of the communities most impacted by a crime ... to repair frayed relationships between neighbours and across borders, and to take the lead in supporting survivors and families impacted by the crime. And it is for this reason that, as we gather today to remember all those who lost their lives at Srebrenica, we must also pause and pay tribute to the many men and women who have done so much in the years that followed the terrible events of 1995 to help us move forward, while at the same time ensuring that we never forget our past.

Srebrenica reminds me of another ICTY appeals case over which I presided, the appeal of General Zdravko Tolimir. General Tolimir was the chief of military intelligence in the Bosnian Serb Army and a leading military commander during the war in Bosnia. For his role in the Srebrenica genocide he was sentenced to imprisonment for life, but he died in 2016 while still in the UN detention centre at The Hague.

In the Tolimir case, the Appeals Chamber noted that while causing serious bodily or mental harm to members of a protected group is one of the enumerated ways in which the crime of genocide can be committed, the ICTR Statute did not explain what qualifies as serious bodily or mental harm. Drawing upon precedents of ICTY trial chambers as well as of the International Court of Justice, the Appeals Chamber recognized that threats of death and knowledge of impending death can amount to serious mental harm for purposes of the crime of genocide, even if the victim survives.

In the Tolimir case, the Appeals Chamber was also called upon to consider a separate type of underlying genocidal act: the deliberate infliction on a protected group of measures calculated to bring about its physical destruction in whole or in part. In its judgment, the court affirmed that this type of genocidal act refers to methods of destruction that do not immediately kill the members of the group, but ultimately seek their physical destruction. Examples of such acts include "subjecting the group to a subsistence diet; failing to provide adequate medical care; systematically expelling members of the group from their homes; and generally creating circumstances that would lead to a slow death such as the lack of proper food, water, shelter, clothing, sanitation, or subjecting members of the group to excessive work or physical exertion". How true. Just think of the thousands of people who died of hunger or typhus in the Warsaw Ghetto.

In the Tolimir case, the Appeals Chamber recognized as well that the victims of the crime of genocide are not only those subjected to specific genocidal acts; rather, as it emphasized, all individuals belonging to the targeted part of the protected group were to be considered victims of the genocide. While holding that the forcible transfer of the population of Žepa by the Bosnian Serb Army did not amount to a genocidal operation, the Appeals Chamber ruled that this did not mean that the Muslim civilians of Žepa were not victims of genocide. It stated that all the members of a protected group were the victims of genocidal acts of killings and causing serious mental harm.

This is a legally meaningful principle, of course, but it is also, I believe, even more than that: it is a ruling of great significance for those who survived the terrible events at issue in that case, for it offers recognition of what genocide means – not just for those who have lost their lives but for entire communities and peoples that were targeted. Thus, under the Tolimir ruling I would have been a victim of genocide even if no member of my family had been killed by the Nazis.

It is perhaps a truism, but this type of recognition matters, as does the ability to call a terrible crime exactly what it is: they matter a great deal. In a radio address delivered in August 1941, two months after Germany's surprise attack on Soviet Russia,

A THOUSAND MIRACLES

Winston Churchill described the atrocities being committed as German troops advanced and referred to them as "a crime without a name". Just a few years later, Raphael Lemkin would give a name to crimes such as these: genocide. Today, of course, we all understand the horror of the term "genocide" and the fundamental condemnation that it brings with it.

In elaborating the law of genocide, the international criminal tribunals also made major contributions to clarifying the genocidal criminality of propaganda for genocide – the sort Joseph Goebbels engaged in, which effectively dehumanized Jews, Roma and communists, among others. I am referring here to the "direct and public incitement to genocide" in the language of Article III(c) of the 1948 UN Convention on Genocide. Direct and public incitement to commit genocide is itself a crime, and it is not necessary to demonstrate that it substantially contributed to the commission of acts of genocide. In other words, as the Appeals Chamber of the Rwandan tribunal made clear, the crime of direct and public incitement to commit genocide is an inchoate offence, punishable even if no act of genocide has resulted. This ruling reflects the reality that the dehumanization of Jews and others through Nazi propaganda was critical to the effectiveness of the Holocaust.

14

SURVIVING THE ACQUITTAL OF GENERAL GOTOVINA

During my four terms as president of the International Criminal Tribunal for the former Yugoslavia (ICTY) and three terms as president of the Residual Mechanism, I chaired many appeals. Most of them resulted in convictions and sentences, sometimes very heavy, while some involved acquittals. None of them triggered as harsh *ad hominem* criticisms by a group of my colleagues and the media as the reversal of the conviction of General Ante Gotovina, who was a national hero of Croatia and arch-villain of Serbia. The case was of major political importance. As the presiding judge of the Appeals Chamber in this case, I was responsible for the proceedings and their outcome.

The events giving rise to the case occurred between July and September 1995. During this time, Croatia initiated a military action called Operation Storm for the purpose of retaking control of the Serb-dominated Krajina region of Croatia, which had declared its independence from Croatia in 1991. Gotovina was a colonel-general in the HV (Croatian Army) during this

A THOUSAND MIRACLES

period and was the operational commander of Operation Storm in the southern portion of the Krajina region.

The Trial Chamber found that Gotovina had contributed to a joint criminal enterprise whose common purpose was to permanently remove the Serb civilian population from the Krajina region. In its judgment of 15 April 2011, the Trial Chamber found Gotovina guilty of both persecution and deportation as crimes against humanity. It also found him guilty of violations of the laws or customs of war. He was sentenced to a single term of twenty-four years of imprisonment.

The gravamen of the case involved the legality of Croatian shelling of four Serb-inhabited towns. The Trial Chamber ruled that by indiscriminate and thus illegal shelling, the Croat forces terrorized the Serb population, forcing the latter to depart and causing their unlawful displacement or deportation. The Trial Chamber determined that illegal shelling was considered to be shelling involving artillery impacts more than 200 metres from a (legitimate) military objective. It applied this yardstick to all the shellings, whatever the range, the weather or the type of artillery used. Artillery impacts within 200 metres of a legitimate target were considered justified, while those more than 200 metres from a legitimate target were considered indiscriminate. Unlawful artillery attacks were thus identified by the Trial Chamber as the primary means for forcing the departure of Serb civilians from Krajina. The chamber found that the towns themselves were treated as targets and that the shelling constituted unlawful attack. Fear of the artillery shelling was the primary and direct cause of the inhabitants' departure. As the indiscriminate shelling was part of a widespread and systematic attack against a civilian population, it constituted deportation as a crime against humanity. The Trial Chamber further found that the unlawful attacks were carried out with discriminatory intent and constituted persecution as crimes against humanity.

SURVIVING THE ACQUITTAL OF GENERAL GOTOVINA

Despite its critical importance, the 200 metres margin of error was not based on expert military evidence and the Trial Chamber did not provide a reasoned opinion as to how it derived the figure. The Appeals Chamber agreed that the 200 metres standard was erroneous, but the majority and minority differed on whatever other, alternative modes of liability should be resorted to on the appeal level. Appeal panels are composed of five judges. In this case, the majority of three, led by me, voted to reverse the conviction and release Gotovina from detention. The judgment was scheduled to be delivered on Friday, 16 November 2012. The normal practice was that dissenting opinions were shared with the panel about a week before delivery. However, in this case I received the dissents only on Thursday evening, the eve of the delivery. Nevertheless, we went ahead and on the Friday the Appeals Chamber announced its conclusion, reversing the decision of the Trial Chamber, entering a verdict of acquittal of Gotovina and ordering his release.

In retrospect, I should have postponed delivery of the judgment when I realized how sharp the dissents were, and reconvened deliberations with the object of seeking a greater measure of common ground. I did not pursue that option because as we had announced the date of delivery of the judgment in advance, there were a great many interested visitors, not to mention the press corps. A delay, which could have been considerable, would have been a bombshell. So we proceeded with the delivery, which was probably a mistake.

This became apparent when in the course of the following year a storm blew up in the media over a letter, leaked to the press, by one of the ICTY judges. Fred Harhoff was an *ad litem* judge, a temporary judge assigned to a given case. On 6 June 2013 he emailed a lengthy letter to fifty-six friends, acquaintances and lawyers in which he was extremely critical of a number of acquittals by the ICTY of military commanders, and singled me out "for tenacious pressure on his colleagues ... to achieve an acquittal". Harhoff asked, "Have any American or Israeli officials ever exerted pressure on the American presiding judge ... to assure a change of directions?" The letter quickly found its way to the Danish newspaper *Berlingske* and other media.

As my Palestinian opinions were widely known, any suggestion that I might yield to Israeli pressure was nonsense. Of course, it is possible that Harhoff did not know about the opinions. And the very idea that US officials would pressure an American who served as an international judge on a judicial matter was equally improbable.

I have always followed the judges' convention of not responding to any criticism, taking stoically whatever stones were thrown my way. My only reaction was an internal memorandum to judges, dated 17 June 213, in which I referred to the publication of the private email of Judge Harhoff and the resulting press stories, "which have unfairly questioned the integrity and the impartiality of the Tribunal's work, and repeated utterly unfounded accusations concerning Tribunal judges, myself included". I concluded by saying that the "Tribunal will continue to discharge its functions faithfully and conscientiously, and as judges and professionals. I have no doubt we will all overcome this difficult time with both dignity and decorum."

On 26 June, Harhoff circulated to the ICTY judges a letter of "unlimited and unconditional apologies". But this letter was not leaked to the media and the public did not hear of it. The damage caused by his first letter was already done.

The media love scandals and I was an easy target. The *New York Times* article by Marlise Simons of 14 June was characteristic of the kind of press attention I received. I have always known that I lack at least one vital leadership quality: a thick skin. So I hurt, in silence.

In 2023, Monique and I spent a week in St Raphael on the Côte d'Azur in a villa belonging to the Legion of Honour.

SURVIVING THE ACQUITTAL OF GENERAL GOTOVINA

The blue sea, the sandy beach, the large balcony with the sea view, dining in the garden at twilight, all of these wonders were largely spoiled for me by the almost daily negative stories about me in the newspapers, attributing to me whatever they could think of.

I felt utterly miserable. I could not sleep and spent my time agonizing. I discussed the situation with Monique. I told her that I must withdraw my candidature for re-election as president and perhaps step down from judgeship of the ICTY. She strongly disagreed. A resignation, she said, would be seen as an admission that I was wrong on Gotovina. "If judges vote you down, go down standing, with a bang, not a whimper." So I maintained my candidature and was re-elected. Monique was right. If you believe in something, stand up and be counted.

I went to the election with a heavy heart. The colleagues who told me that they would vote for me were a majority, but you can never know what people will do in a secret ballot. Still, since the judges who opposed me, while probably in a minority, were vocal and a bit intimidating, it was the secret ballot that gave me a chance.

As a candidate, I could not chair the plenary, as I usually did, and asked one of the past presidents, Patrick Robinson from Jamaica, to serve as the acting president for the meeting. The atmosphere was toxic. Elections of presidents are usually conducted calmly and efficiently. But this was not a typical election. It was a sharp contest. One of the judges broke the unwritten rule that one may praise but not denigrate a candidate, and started a personal tirade against me until cut short by Robinson. Robinson said: "I have exceptionally allowed you to speak in the interest of a democratic procedure, but I have to say that the whole tone of your speech is really unprecedented. I have been here from 1998. I have participated in all the elections, and I have never heard a statement of this kind."

A THOUSAND MIRACLES

My opponent was nominated in a glowing and long statement by the Russian judge. I was nominated in one short sentence by the British judge. In the atmosphere of the room, even a whisper in my favour took courage. The secret ballots were distributed by the Australian registrar, John Hocking, and quickly counted. The vote was twelve to six in my favour.

I took the floor briefly and said: "I am deeply honoured that my colleagues elected me for a second term as president ... I would like to assure all colleagues that I appreciate fully the need to restore collegiality and that the vice-president and I are committed to ensuring that we lead our colleagues towards the restoration of a harmonious working environment for all judges and staff in these difficult times of down-sizing."

Harhoff was a judge on a panel sitting in judgment on a Serb defendant, Vojislav Šešelj. On 9 July 2013, Šešelj filed a motion seeking the disqualification of Harhoff on the basis that Harhoff's leaked letter gave rise to a reasonable fear of bias in favour of convictions in the proceedings in which he was involved. The motion further argued that the letter showed a strong inclination on the part of Harhoff to convict accused persons of Serbian ethnicity.

As I had to recuse myself, the vice-president appointed a panel of three judges to rule on the motion. With one dissent, the panel found that in his letter Judge Harhoff had "demonstrated a bias in favour of a conviction such that a reasonable observer properly informed would reasonably apprehend bias. As such an acceptable appearance of bias exists." The motion was upheld. Since this was the only case to which Harhoff was assigned, the disqualification was his swansong as an international judge of the ICTY. Had he not been disqualified and stayed on, he might eventually have been assigned another case. Thus the sanction was significant. So the whole story did not end well for Harhoff,

SURVIVING THE ACQUITTAL OF GENERAL GOTOVINA

as it cost him his judicial job. Although I was his target and suffered harm, I could not help feeling sorry for him.

But even during the most difficult times, most governments were reasonably supportive. Among the permanent members of the Security Council, France, the United Kingdom and the United States were friendly, and I could normally count on the sympathy of China. Only Russian diplomats, with rare exceptions, were difficult, perhaps because of Russia's close ties with Serbia and perhaps because they considered me too independent. But British officials followed proceedings in the ICTY closely and were certainly the best informed and the most knowledgeable. They understood that international criminal tribunals were not about convictions; they were about justice.

I will never forget a brief meeting during the height of the Harhoff controversy. Monique and I were attending a wedding of a friend in the gardens of the Inns of Court in London. The weather and the setting were wonderful, and the London summer was at its very best. But I was utterly demoralized. And then out of the blue Iain Macleod (now Sir Iain), the highly respected legal adviser of the Foreign Office, came over to me and said: "Ted, I can see you are feeling down. But do remember, you are not a pariah, you are a leader of men." Even at the best of times, this would have been good to hear. During the worst of times, it was a wonderful tonic.

The story of the court proceedings regarding Gotovina did not end with the judgment of the Appeals Chamber. In the genocide case of Croatia against Serbia in the International Court of Justice (ICJ), the counsel for Serbia challenged the ICTY appeal judgment. While the ICJ has no hierarchical or line authority over the ICTY, as the principal judicial organ of the United Nations its findings are of course of great importance. The ICJ thus decided to consider the complaints of Serbia against the ICTY judgment over which I presided. In a detailed judgment given on 3 February 2015, the ICJ clearly agreed with the Appeals Chamber:

> 472. The Court concludes from the foregoing that it is unable to find that there was any indiscriminate shelling of the Krajina towns deliberately intended to cause civilian casualties. It would only be in exceptional circumstances that it would depart from the findings reached by the ICTY on an issue of this kind. Serbia has indeed drawn the Court's attention to the controversy aroused by the Appeals Chamber's Judgment. However, no evidence, whether prior or subsequent to that Judgment, has been put before the Court which would incontrovertibly show that the Croatian authorities deliberately intended to shell the civilian areas inhabited by Serbs. In particular, no such intent is apparent from the Brioni transcript ... Nor can such intent be regarded as incontrovertibly established on the basis of the statements by persons having testified before the ICTY Trial Chamber in the Gotovina case, and cited as witnesses by Serbia in the present case.

These conclusions by the ICJ effectively put an end to the public and the academic controversy about the reversal of Gotovina's conviction. But the ICJ stepped in as late as February 2015, more than two years after the ICTY Appeals Chamber judgment of November 2012. For me, these two years were clearly *anni horribiles*.

Looking back at these events after a decade, I thank God for helping me through. I am grateful for the support of the majority of my colleagues in the ICTY presidential elections. A vote for my opponent would have been seen as rebuking me for Gotovina. I was lucky that Serbia complained against the Gotovina acquittal in the ICJ, creating an opportunity for the principal judicial organ of the United Nations to pronounce on this matter and give its unanimous imprimatur to our majority judgment.

Though wounded and hurt, I emerged from these events grateful that I had stood up for justice, even when it meant going against the current.

15

OXFORD REDUX

Since my visiting fellowships at All Souls in 1989 and 1991, I had been daydreaming of returning to Oxford on a more permanent basis. I spoke about my interest in Oxford to my NYU colleague and friend Philip Alston, a prominent human rights scholar and activist who knew people at the Oxford Law Faculty, and asked him to let them know of my interest. This must have had an impact as in 2014 I was contacted by two members of the faculty, Catherine Redgwell, the Chichele Professor of Public International Law, and Dapo Akande, a rising star in international law and, from 2023, Catherine's successor when she retired. We agreed to meet for lunch at the Oxford and Cambridge Club in London.

At our meeting, Catherine said that international criminal law was not being taught in Oxford and asked whether I would be interested in introducing it to the programme and teaching it. I agreed, enthusiastically. I made it clear that I did not want to be compensated and that any honorarium should be credited to international criminal law scholarships in the faculty. Eventually, I also donated some additional money and established a fellowship to enable a student from the Oxford Law Faculty to act as an intern at one of the war crimes tribunals in The Hague. Some years later, after moving to Trinity College, I also established a number of prizes and scholarships in law and in literature there. This was my way of giving back to Oxford, which is so dear to my heart.

I started teaching a seminar on international criminal law with my colleague and friend Miles Jackson. Our seminars were held in the lovely Old Library at All Souls. After some years, commercial and private law courses gained interest among the students, due perhaps to the greater prospects of higher earnings, and so we noticed a decline in students taking international criminal law. This led unfortunately to the termination of the seminar. Even now, however, I still have a weekly research seminar for postgraduate law students, and some doctoral and master's examinations, which keep me busy while leaving me enough time for occasional public lectures and writing.

When I first joined the faculty, I was still a full-time appeals judge and president of both the ICTY and the Residual Mechanism. So I would come to Oxford on Thursday evenings, teach on Friday and travel back to The Hague at the weekend.

During my first few years in Oxford, All Souls granted me honorary membership of the Senior Common Room with some dining rights. Eventually, the arrangements at All Souls came to an end, but Trinity came to the rescue. During my occasional stays in Trinity I met its president, Sir Ivor Roberts, who as the past UK ambassador to Belgrade was interested in my ICTY work. Over time we became good friends. After a while, he nominated me for honorary membership of the Trinity Senior Common Room, which meant that I could dine and meet fellows there. Eventually, under the presidency of Dame Hilary Boulding, I was promoted to visiting honorary fellow and, a couple of years later, honorary fellow. Trinity thus became my home, where

OXFORD REDUX

I spend the academic year. An honorary fellow is in effect an appointment for life. And the Law Faculty was good enough to continue reappointing me as a visiting professor of law in three-year cycles, most recently until September 2026.

In Trinity I have been fortunate to live in the top-floor Chavasse suit. Noel Chavasse was a medical captain who in World War I was awarded the Victoria Cross twice. He fell on the battlefield in 1917. My staircase was designed by Sir Christopher Wren, the architect of St Paul's Cathedral. From my windows I have a great view of the gardens and the spires of St John's College and Wadham College. How lucky can one be!

Additional opportunities opened up. Kate O'Regan, past justice in the South African Constitutional Court, invited me to become an academic associate of the Bonavero Human Rights Institute, of which she is the director, and Helen Mountfield, principal of Mansfield College, invited me to be a visiting fellow there. I have also given sermons and lectures on the Holocaust at Trinity and All Souls.

For me, to spend time in Oxford as an academic was like a dream come true. I found truly fascinating my conversations with colleagues, usually during meals in college, each from a different discipline, about most of which I was totally uninformed. I equally enjoyed talking to Trinity students, usually in the garden or the courtyards. They come from so many different social and economic backgrounds, are touchingly happy to have made it to Oxford, and are surprisingly willing to spend time chatting with a dinosaur about their concerns, lives and hopes. I find my involvement with students invigorating and perhaps even rejuvenating.

The other aspects of Oxford that I love so much are its architecture, its natural beauty and, of course, its music. I sometimes think that Oxford has more classical music performances than many large cities. Monique and I particularly enjoyed going to listen to Bach cantatas in the New College Chapel on Sunday afternoons. It is a pity the wonderful Bach choir did not resume performing after the Covid lockdown.

Monique loved Oxford and came from time to time for a weekend or a special event, as when I had to give a public talk. With her I used to walk to the river and watch the boats practise. Or we would cross the river and stroll to Iffley Lock and then have a Sunday roast in the Prince of Wales. When Monique died, one of my friends in Trinity, Sue Broers, wrote in a message of condolence that Trinity would be my second home. In fact, it has become my first home, as I spend the entire academic year there.

∞

Prior to my UN General Assembly Holocaust commemoration speech in 2020, which I have discussed in the opening chapter of this book, I was not comfortable speaking about the Holocaust and did my best to avoid doing so. But that speech helped me to exorcise my Holocaust demons and I no longer treat the Holocaust as a taboo subject. It was my work on that speech as well as several sermons I have given at Trinity and All Souls that made me reflect on the role of the bystander as an enabler of the Holocaust.

Let me share with you my reflections on the subject of the bystander in the Holocaust, in contrast to the Good Samaritan. I define a bystander as someone who was aware of the harm to which persecuted Jews were exposed, but who nonetheless looked away or chose not to act. The Good Samaritan is one who complies with a duty to help others, so long as they take on no major risk themselves. (I realize that these categories are fluid and interchangeable, rather than static.)

Murders on the scale of the Holocaust are not possible when an entire society stands up for the rule of law, human dignity, and equality for all. The murder of six million Jews would not have been possible without the acquiescence, if not complicity, of the peoples of Germany and occupied Europe. In other words, the Holocaust could not have happened without those who had a good idea of the harm being perpetrated but who averted their eyes and did and said nothing.

As a collective, bystanders bear a heavy moral responsibility. What is more difficult to assess in the abstract, however, is the moral responsibility of each individual bystander. Bystanders may be involved in various ways – through acquiescence, complicity or participation – and each corresponds to a different and increasing degree of moral responsibility. Every person's situational circumstances, such as knowledge, proximity and ability to help, must be taken into account in assessing responsibility.

In rare cases during the war, would-be bystanders banded together and rejected complicity with the Holocaust as immoral and, as a result, Jews were saved. Why, then, in most cases did majorities stand by? There are a number of reasons. The fear of German retribution against the rescuer and his or her family was a major factor. It was not only the rescuer who faced the danger of the death penalty, but also the protester who faced the heavy risk of Nazi retribution. And while the French archbishop Pierre-Marie Gerlier and a number of French bishops made statements in support of Jews and were not punished by the Nazi occupiers, this did not provide adequate reassurance for lower-ranking priests or private individuals. But they did encourage French monasteries to give shelter to Jews.

So what then motivated bystanders to be bystanders? There was the antisemitism so effectively disseminated by the Goebbels propaganda machine, and yet this is an incomplete explanation. After all, a country as antisemitic as Poland then was had the highest number of those who risked their lives to save Jews in proportion to the population as a whole.

A THOUSAND MIRACLES

Another motivation was the social stigma attached to Jews, which discouraged others from speaking up on their behalf. There was, too, the satisfaction of getting rid of perceived competition or persons who were often different and resented or envied by the majority. For some, there was even sadistic joy in getting rid of Jews. There was the Catholic Church, with its great influence, which often espoused antisemitic sentiment and was for the most part conspicuously silent in the face of Jewish suffering. There was also the tradition of respect for and obedience to authority and leadership, even to manifestly unjust and brutal laws. This was a major factor for compliance in Germany and even in a country as historically friendly to Jews as the Netherlands. There was the prospect of material advantage, as multitudes benefited from assets, businesses and apartments left behind by Jews. Finally, there was the ubiquitous tendency to turn away from the person in need.

The biblical story of the Good Samaritan is inextricably linked with the duty to love one's neighbour. The parable is not neutral as to who acted justly when faced with someone in great need, but rather clearly favours the Samaritan and compassionate mercy. At the same time, it says nothing about the victim and his ethnicity or religion. By making the victim anonymous, the parable makes proximity and identity irrelevant to our duties towards universal humanity.

Is the Good Samaritan a model for those who helped Jews to escape death in the Holocaust? Yes and no. Yes, as the parable promotes the universal version of the duty to love one's neighbour and to take appropriate action. A Christian must love all humans, including Jews. But also no. The relevance of the parable is not complete, as the Good Samaritan does not risk his own life for his neighbour, as those who tried to rescue victims of the Holocaust did. If we think of a Good Samaritan as a person taking on a risk-free or low-risk action, as distinct from risking their own life, then we must accept that it was extremely difficult to be a Good Samaritan during the Holocaust. Those who aided Jews faced harsh punishment. Most people were bystanders, unwilling even to protest.

Perhaps the best-known example of Good Samaritans during the Holocaust was the people of Denmark. They transported all Danish Jews to Sweden in an extraordinary human rescue operation during the dark days of the war. How can we explain the Danes' willingness to act as Good Samaritans? The thoroughgoing participation of the Danish people, combined with leadership from the King down, most likely reduced the real and perceived risk faced by individual Danes, as they acted within a broader culture of resistance which provided protection from betrayal and punishment.

∞

One thing I would never have dared to expect was the Oxford Law Faculty workshop in my honour hosted jointly by All Souls and Trinity in June 2024. Two panels consisted of younger scholars presenting their research projects. The third panel consisted of three brilliant people with whom I had worked closely during my professional career: Jean Galbraith, my past law clerk and now a professor of law at Penn Law School; Emiliya Viktorova, with whom I have worked on many cases; and Shehzad Charania, a senior Foreign Office lawyer and past legal adviser of the British Embassy in The Hague. Shehzad spoke eloquently of my Palestine opinions, and my role in the Gotovina case and in defence of Judge Akay, as examples of my commitment to judicial independence.

I would like to take the liberty of ending this chapter by quoting from Jean's address, which presented a comprehensive picture of my professional life.

A THOUSAND MIRACLES

My task here is to speak about the arc of Ted's scholarly career. For this task, I received two inputs. First, at my request, Ted provided me with a "selected" list of his publications. It included 11 books, 3 edited volumes, 23 book chapters, 40 articles or comments in the *American Journal of International Law*, for which he served as editor-in-chief for many years, 49 other articles, and 13 miscellaneous publications. It is astounding, to say the least, that almost all that prodigious work that I mentioned earlier was written after Ted became a full-time academic *at the age of 48*.

When I think of Ted's scholarship, I divide it, broadly speaking, into four eras.

Era One is Ted as the Restless Generalist. To be clear, we've never left the era of Ted as a generalist – more on that later – but in his academic work in the 1970s and early 1980s, Ted takes his incredible energy and channels it into everything he finds interesting. And he finds lots of things interesting ...

Era Two is Ted as the Human Rights Scholar. After becoming a professor at NYU, Ted was asked to teach a regular human rights course. During the 1980s, he became a giant in the field ... In this era, Ted also writes *Human Rights in Internal Strife*, which is a compelling argument for the need for core non-derogable principles to fill the gap between human rights law and international humanitarian law – a gap that arises in situations of strife where human rights protections are absent because of derogation and where international humanitarian law protections are absent because the strife does not rise to the level of an armed conflict. He also writes his book on *Human Rights and Humanitarian Norms as Customary International Law* ...

Era Three is Ted as the Magisterial Generalist. In the 1990s and onward, Ted takes all his existing interests, develops new ones, and weaves them together into an account of law and humanity. He unearths the deep roots of these themes through his work on the laws of war and chivalry in the Middle Ages and their exploration in Shakespeare's histories ... Ted writes two books and many articles in this space, engaging closely not just with Shakespeare, but also with the work of numerous medieval writers and scholars like Alberico Gentili and Christine de Pisan.

Then, in his 2003 Hague General Course and his subsequent book, *The Humanization of International Law*, Ted produces what he calls "the book that is closest to reflecting the quintessence of my work". He explores the influence that human rights law has had and is having across many fields of public international law. He shows, powerfully, how international law is moving away from reciprocity and towards humanity, away from a state-centric perspective and more towards a focus on individuals.

Finally, in the Fourth Era, which overlaps with Era Three and continues today, Ted focuses increasingly on international criminal law. Much of his work draws from his experience as a Judge ... I'll note that, well before he went on the bench, Ted's important work included (a) an article calling for the creation of the ICTY; (b) a comment on the importance of prosecuting rape as a war crime; and (c) an article, written before the *Tadic* decision, arguing that violations of ... Article III of the Geneva Conventions amount to war crimes under customary international law for non-international armed conflicts ...

Let me turn now to themes – beyond the obvious themes of Ted as a generalist, as an endlessly curious intellectual, and as an unstoppable force of nature ...

The American mathematician Richard Hamming once gave a famous talk called "You and Your Research". He described how, when he would meet scholars in other fields, he would ask: "what are the important problems in your field?" And his follow-up question would be: "Are *you* working on these problems?" He wasn't entirely popular, for his questions were meant as a test – a test that Ted and his work pass with flying colours.

As I think about the Meron canon, I see it as tackling two questions of critical importance in our field and in the world – questions that sound straightforward and yet that hold the keys to the kingdom, if we can only get there.

A THOUSAND MIRACLES

The first is this: how can we progressively develop international law to reduce human suffering? Almost all of Ted's work is devoted to answering this question. He has been a ceaseless advocate for the expansion of human rights principles. He has championed developments in international humanitarian law that will bring more protections to individuals and advances in international criminal law that increase accountability for perpetrators ...

The second core inquiry I see in the Meron canon is this: how do we build commitment to an ethos of humanity? You can find this theme in Ted's work as early as his study of the UN Secretariat, and it builds throughout all four eras. It is reflected in his perpetual interest in the Martens Clause [which appeared in the preamble to the 1899 Hague Convention]. Above all, it is present in his writings on chivalry, which he uses to illustrate the need for collective and individual commitment to integrity and humanism.

Ted writes: "The humane and noble ideals of chivalry included justice and loyalty, courage, honour and mercy, the obligations not to kill or otherwise take advantage of the vanquished enemy and to keep one's word ... the duties to protect the weak, ... to help people in distress, ... to redress wrongs, to avenge injustice" and "to act nobly and generously". That is Ted's description of chivalry. It also sounds remarkably like Ted.

And that is my final point: that Ted is not only a legendary scholar; he is also a legend who lives his scholarship.

16

FROM THE BENCH TO THE BAR
PROSECUTING UKRAINE AND GAZA WAR CRIMES

My appointment in June 2022 as special adviser of the prosecutor of the ICC on international humanitarian law marked my return, at the age of ninety-two, to practical involvement in international criminal justice, this time not as a judge but as a prosecutor. This meant I would look at the case before me from the perspective of one party, the prosecutor, and not from the centre, as a judge. I was happy to have been considered as someone who at my age could still contribute to the creation of a world in which accountability is at least an expectation, and I gladly accepted. There was only one caveat in my acceptance. In a brief telephone conversation with Prosecutor Karim Khan, I said that I would have to recuse myself from cases involving Israel–Palestine. Karim agreed. He had appeared before me as a counsel for the defence or appellants in a number of appeals over which I presided in UN war crimes tribunals. I found him impressive, effective and courteous. In short, I liked him. And after so many years on the bench, I was curious about being part of the Office of the Prosecution.

∞

One of the major issues in the Ukraine war was the very fact of the Russian invasion of that country in February 2022, which was defined as aggression by the majority of the UN General Assembly. This was not only a critical development in terms of the principle of accountability, but something of a wake-up call for international criminal justice. The war showed once again the central importance of the ICC. For the Russian invasion was a type of deliberate war resorted to by a major power, a permanent member of the UN Security Council, that we had hoped, even assumed, would not happen again, certainly not in Europe.

Although the vote of the General Assembly against Russia was certainly strong and persuasive, it was not universal. Many Third World countries preferred not to take sides and to abstain. While I agree that the invasion and the war constituted aggression and merits prosecution of the Russian leadership, I will not deal with it here because I did not work on the matter in the ICC. Instead I will discuss the two issues that I did in fact work on: the deportation of Ukrainian children to Russia and some of the Gaza crimes.

∞

In contrast to the crime of aggression, the jurisdiction of the ICC with regard to the deportation of children from Ukraine is clear, as the crimes were committed on the territory of a state that accepted the jurisdiction of the ICC. On 8 September 2015, the registrar of the ICC received a declaration lodged by Ukraine accepting the ICC's jurisdiction with respect to alleged crimes committed in its territory since 20 February 2014. The

FROM THE BENCH TO THE BAR

declaration was lodged under Article 12(3) of the Rome Statute, the founding treaty of the ICC, which enables a state not party to the Statute to accept the exercise of jurisdiction of the court.

This is the second declaration under Article 12(3) of the Statute lodged by Ukraine. On 17 April 2014, Ukraine lodged a declaration under the same article accepting the jurisdiction of the ICC over alleged crimes committed on its territory from 21 November 2013 to 22 February 2014. Both declarations mention crimes against humanity and war crimes, but not genocide. The national law of Ukraine contains the crime of aggression.

On 17 March 2023 Pre-trial Chamber II of the ICC, following requests from Prosecutor Khan, issued warrants of arrest for President Vladimir Putin of Russia and Mrs Maria Lvova-Belova, the Russian commissioner for children's rights, for the war crime of unlawful deportation of children from Ukraine to the Russian Federation. On the same day, the ICC prosecutor issued a statement (see below) which revealed additional elements of importance. Many of the deported children had been adopted by Russian families and given Russian nationality despite their status as protected persons under the Geneva Conventions.

> Incidents identified by my Office include the deportation of at least hundreds of children taken from orphanages and children's care homes. Many of these children, we allege, have since been given for adoption in the Russian Federation. The law was changed in the Russian Federation, through Presidential decrees issued by President Putin, to expedite the conferral of Russian citizenship, making it easier for them to be adopted by Russian families.
>
> My Office alleges that these acts, amongst others, demonstrate an intention to permanently remove these children from their own country. At the time of these deportations, the Ukrainian children were protected persons under the Fourth Geneva Convention.
>
> In September last year, I addressed the United Nations Security Council and emphasised that the investigation of alleged illegal

deportation of children from Ukraine was a priority for my Office. The human impact of these crimes was also made clear during my most recent visit to Ukraine. While there, I visited one of the care homes from which children were allegedly taken, close to the current frontlines of the conflict. The accounts of those who had cared for these children, and their fears as to what had become of them, underlined the urgent need for action.

We must ensure that those responsible for alleged crimes are held accountable and that children are returned to their families and communities. As I stated at the time, we cannot allow children to be treated as if they are the spoils of war.

As someone who was a child during World War II in occupied Poland, I am particularly touched by the plight of the deported children and their families, from which they would typically be separated. The legal situation concerning these violations of the Geneva Conventions is clear. Since the arrest warrants issued are still confidential, the following analysis is my own.

The principal basis for my discussion is the general prohibition of forcible transfers and deportations of protected persons from occupied territory to the territory of the occupying power, as stated in Article 49(1) of the Fourth Geneva Convention. This prohibition is categorical and applies to all protected persons in occupied territory, whether children or not. Russia claims that these transfers or evacuations have been voluntary. However, leaving aside the veracity of these claims, under the Geneva Conventions renunciations of rights of protected persons are invalid. This prohibition on the renunciation of rights is absolute and inalienable. Its inclusion in Article 8 of the Fourth Convention was triggered by the experience of pressure exercised during World War II on inhabitants of territories occupied by Nazi Germany to waive some of their rights under the Hague Regulations of 1907.

FROM THE BENCH TO THE BAR

Regimes of occupation are by their very nature coercive and make suspect any consent to renunciation or waiver of rights of protected persons. In any event, consent to the transfer of children to Russian territory cannot be given by minors. There is an exception to the prohibition on forcible deportations, also stated in Article 49, allowing partial or total evacuation of a given area if the security of the population or imperative military reasons so demand. But such evacuations may not involve the displacement of protected persons "outside the bounds of the occupied territory" "except when for material reasons". In cases where temporary transfers outside occupied territory are allowed, the evacuees should be returned to their country as soon as hostilities have ceased in their area and families should be kept together. This provision, too, appears to have been breached by Russia.

The allegations that Russian authorities have facilitated the adoption of Ukrainian children by families in Russia and conferred Russian passports on Ukrainian children, if true, would amount to violations of the provisions of Article 50(2) of Geneva Convention IV, which states that the occupying power "may not, in any case, change their [the protected persons'] personal status". As I see it, both adoption and Russian naturalization change the personal status of children. Since granting Russian nationality must have been approved at a very high level, I would think that civilian and military authorities of high rank could be charged (as indeed they were). In short, the case against Russia is strong.

∞

In March 2024, during the long spring break in Oxford, I was in New York to teach a seven-week seminar at the NYU Law School. On Friday, 22 March, my mobile phone rang. It was Karim Khan. He said he remembered that upon my appointment

A THOUSAND MIRACLES

as special adviser on international humanitarian law, we had agreed that I would recuse myself from any involvement in cases concerning Israel–Palestine. But the current war in Gaza required him to appoint a small group of international law experts to advise him on the possibility of issuing arrest warrants for leaders of the warring parties who had allegedly committed crimes against humanity and war crimes. Members of the group would appreciate my joining them and had asked him to approach me. Could I waive my recusal plan?

I told him that I would rather he had not approached me, but once he did, it would be hypocritical of me to decline. How could someone who had served on and led UN war crimes tribunals for about twenty years say no? So I said yes and the following day flew to Amsterdam. On my arrival at The Hague, a staff member of the ICC was waiting for me with thick files – my urgent reading material.

On Monday morning I was present at the ICC for a meeting of the experts, six altogether, assisted by the staff of the Prosecution Office. I spent a whole week in the ICC, having rescheduled two sessions of my NYU seminar. Our work continued with person-to-person meetings in London after my return from New York to Oxford and more intensive virtual consultations and drafting. Eventually, we issued a report of our panel on 20 May 2024 and on the same day published a joint op-ed article in the *Financial Times* of London. I found the group highly qualified, fair, cohesive and friendly.

Financial Times, 20 May 2024

> Why We Support ICC Prosecutions for Crimes in Israel and Gaza
> The attacks by Hamas in Israel on October 7 and the military response by Israeli forces in Gaza have tested the system of

FROM THE BENCH TO THE BAR

international law to its limits. This is why, as international lawyers, we felt compelled to assist when the prosecutor of the International Criminal Court, Karim Khan, asked us to advise whether there was sufficient evidence to lay charges of war crimes and crimes against humanity. Today, the prosecutor has taken a historic step to ensure justice for the victims in Israel and Palestine by issuing applications for five arrest warrants alleging war crimes and crimes against humanity by senior Hamas and Israeli leaders. These include applications for a warrant of arrest against the political and military commanders of Hamas and Israeli Prime Minister Benjamin Netanyahu.

For months, we have engaged in an extensive process of review and analysis. We have carefully examined each of the applications for arrest warrants, as well as underlying material produced by the prosecution team in support of the applications. This has included witness statements, expert evidence, official communications, videos and photographs. In our legal report published today, we unanimously agree that the prosecutor's work was rigorous, fair and grounded in the law and the facts. And we unanimously agree that there are reasonable grounds to believe that the suspects he identifies have committed war crimes and crimes against humanity within the jurisdiction of the ICC. It is not unusual for the prosecutor to invite external experts to participate in an evidence-review, under appropriate confidentiality arrangements, during the course of an investigation or trial. And this is not the first time an international prosecutor has formed a Panel of Experts to advise on potential charges related to a conflict. But this conflict is perhaps unprecedented in the extent to which it has given rise to misunderstandings about the ICC's role and jurisdiction, a particularly fractured discourse and, in some contexts, even antisemitism and Islamophobia.

It is against this backdrop that, as lawyers specialised in international law hailing from diverse personal backgrounds, we felt we had a duty to accept the invitation to provide an impartial and independent legal opinion based on evidence. We were selected because of our expertise in public international law, international human rights law, international humanitarian law and international criminal law, and, in the case of two of us, experience as former judges of international criminal tribunals. Our common goal is advancing accountability and we have reached our conclusions based on an assessment of the warrant applications against an objective legal standard. We have reached these conclusions unanimously. And we believe it is important to publish them given the extent to which discourse has been politicised, disinformation has been rife and international media has been denied access to the front lines.

The Panel unanimously agrees with the prosecutor's conclusion that there are reasonable grounds to believe that three of Hamas's most senior leaders – Yahya Sinwar, Mohammed Deif and Ismail Haniyeh – have committed war crimes and crimes against humanity for the killing of hundreds of civilians, the taking of at least 245 hostages and acts of sexual violence committed against Israeli hostages. The Panel also unanimously agrees that the evidence presented by the prosecutor provides reasonable grounds to believe that Netanyahu and Israel's minister of defence Yoav Gallant have committed war crimes and crimes against humanity. This includes the war crime of intentionally using starvation of civilians as a method of warfare and the murder and persecution of Palestinians as crimes against humanity. Our reasons for reaching these conclusions are set out in our legal report.

It is important to understand that the charges have nothing to do with the reasons for the conflict. The charges concern waging war in a manner that violates the long-established rules of international law that apply to armed groups and the armed forces in every state in the world. And, of course, the warrant applications announced today are just the first step. We hope that the prosecutor will continue to conduct focused investigations including in relation to the extensive harm suffered by civilians as a result of the bombing campaign in Gaza and evidence of sexual violence committed against Israelis on October 7. There is no doubt that the step taken today by the prosecutor is a milestone in the history of international criminal law. There is no conflict that should be excluded from the reach of the law; no child's life valued less than another's. The law we apply is humanity's law, not the law of any given side. It must protect all the victims of this conflict; and all civilians in conflicts to come. The judges of the ICC will ultimately determine which warrants, if any, should be issued. And as investigations continue, we hope that state authorities, witnesses and survivors will engage with the judicial process. Ultimately, we hope that this process will contribute to increased protections for civilians and sustainable peace in a region that has already endured too much.

Lord Justice Fulford, retired lord justice of appeal, former vice-president of the Court of Appeal of England and Wales and former judge at the International Criminal Court

Judge Theodor Meron CMG, visiting professor at the University of Oxford, honorary fellow, Trinity College, and former judge and former president of the International Criminal Tribunal for the former Yugoslavia

Amal Clooney, barrister, adjunct professor at Columbia Law School and co-founder of the Clooney Foundation for Justice

Danny Friedman KC, barrister, expert in criminal law, international law and human rights

Baroness Helena Kennedy LT KC, barrister, member of the House of Lords and director of the International Bar Association Human Rights Institute

Elizabeth Wilmshurst CMG KC, former deputy legal adviser at the United Kingdom Foreign and Commonwealth Office and distinguished fellow of international law at Chatham House

A THOUSAND MIRACLES

In our full report we elaborated some critical points. Thus, we agreed that the ICC had jurisdiction in relation to crimes committed on the territory of Palestine, including Gaza, and over crimes committed by Palestinian nationals inside or outside Palestine territory. It also had jurisdiction over Palestinian nationals who committed crimes on the territory of Israel. We agreed that the prosecutor could seek arrest warrants of three senior Hamas leaders for the war crimes of murder and the crimes against humanity of murder and extermination for the killing of hundreds of civilians on 7 October 2023, and for taking at least 245 persons hostage and for the war crimes of rape and other forms of sexual violence and torture, and for the crimes against humanity of rape and other forms of sexual violence committed against Israeli hostages while they were in captivity. The three Hamas leaders had since been killed.

We agreed further that the prosecutor could seek arrest warrants against Israeli prime minister Benjamin Netanyahu and minister of defence Yoav Gallant for committing the war crime of using starvation as a method of warfare and for the crimes against humanity of murder, extermination and persecution with regard to the systematic deprivation of means indispensable to the survival of Palestinian civilians in Gaza.

As could be expected, we received both praise and harsh criticism. I was used to plenty of criticism in my role as president of UN war crimes tribunals. Criticism is never pleasant, but for me it was always almost part of my job description. In this case public criticism was directed in large part against the British-Lebanese lawyer Amal Clooney and me. I was in good company.

Of course, the prosecutor has considerable discretion regarding the timing and the contents of the charges he chooses to present. Prosecutor Khan was harshly criticized for presenting to the judges arrest warrants against Israeli ministers and Hamas leaders of a terrorist organization at the same time, and thus making the charges and the accused comparable or similar. Critics argued there is no moral equivalence between the accused of the two parties. I agree, but had the prosecutor submitted charges at different times against the accused of the two parties, he would have been criticized for bias towards one of the parties. I think that by the simultaneous presentation of charges against both parties he did not intend to relativize or analogize the culpability of the perpetrators. He needed time to properly prepare the charges and await evidence for the crimes committed by Hamas. He wanted to show that he was acting according to the requirements of the law and the evidence.

On 6 February 2025, President Trump of the United States issued an executive order entitled "Imposing Sanctions on the International Criminal Court". This was no less than a bombshell for the ICC. The sanctions are harsh and comprehensive and, if maintained for a longer time, threaten not only the functioning but the very survival of the ICC. They will promote impunity for the crimes of genocide, crimes against humanity and war crimes. They will criminalize giving advice to the prosecutor and thus the very function of special advisers to the prosecutor. Of course, the order per se is not retroactive, and the work of the expert group was carried out when no sanction regime was in effect. But the order makes the future of international criminal justice and the work of the ICC quite uncertain and unstable, and undermines the global prospects of accountability. Since the US executive order criminalizes the giving of services – and, thus, advice – to the prosecutor, sadly I was compelled to terminate my contract with the prosecutor as special adviser on international humanitarian law on 7 March 2025.

17

PLEASE DO NOT LEAVE ME

I end this memoir with the most painful days of my life, the parting from Monique. I had a rough childhood, losing my mother, brother and most of my family to the Holocaust. Perhaps it was the chaos of wartime, perhaps my emotional reserves had been drained or the survival instinct was too dominating, but the pain of losing my family was nothing compared with the shock, grief, despair and total loneliness I felt when Monique left me. For the first time she was not there to soothe me when I needed her most, to share my thoughts, to talk to and hear her voice. Perhaps this is the price one must pay for true love. Nothing could be greater than the years with her.

Defying superstition, we married on Friday, 13 March 1981, in the town hall of Grand-Saconnex in Geneva, where we later bought a house. In the civil marriage ceremony, the Swiss officiant read what was still a very patriarchal and outdated formula based on the Swiss Civil Code of 1907, which we found quite amusing: the husband is the head of the family and the wife takes care of the household and helps him with care and advice. This certainly did not fit my relationship with Monique.

A THOUSAND MIRACLES

When we met, she was forty-six, I was fifty. We were no longer youngsters. I had always believed in the equality of the sexes and full and equal partnership in marriage. Monique, from a French Huguenot family, had a successful career of her own as a linguist, translator and reviser in the United Nations, and it was clear that we would each continue in our different professional activities. Our totally different backgrounds and career interests were not an impediment and, in retrospect, could even have been a stimulus for an exceptional relationship.

This was the beginning of a charmed life of love, partnership and mutual support, which lasted more than forty-two years. She loved travelling and went twice on the Silk Route. Whenever possible she travelled with me to conferences and lectures and, of course, on vacations. We went together to Rome for the establishment of the ICC, to Alaska to watch bears catching salmon, to Antarctica, Abu Dhabi, the Hanseatic cities on the Baltic, the Falls of Iguazu in Argentina, and to castles, monasteries and particularly cloisters, in which we shared an almost fanatical interest. We both loved the sea and went many times to the coasts of Brittany and Normandy, as well as to Cape Cod. Her enthusiasm was enormous and her stamina inexhaustible.

The last few years of her life were not easy. She suffered from a strong and recurrent vertigo, falling several times and fracturing limbs and once her pelvis, and was rapidly losing her sight. At the end she was practically blind. But she never complained and soldiered on. I tried to look for solutions which could enable her to remain as independent as possible: gadgets to facilitate reading, arrangements for vocally rendering texts on the computer, an immense TV. Nothing seemed to work or catch up with the rapid deterioration.

Because of my Oxford and other commitments, she was mostly alone in our Paris apartment despite her many friends. She was always radiant when I came to Paris every weekend or two. We would go shopping and for walks, holding hands like children. As time went on, owing to blindness, it was difficult for her to walk without support. She gradually slowed down and led a more sedentary life until she seldom went out. She was fiercely independent and she never wanted me to stay in Paris to assist her. I cannot express the warmth I felt for her.

Whether I was in Oxford, New York or elsewhere, we spoke many times a day on the phone, sharing everything about our activities, thoughts, feelings. I offered – perhaps not insisting enough – to step down from Oxford and spend all my time with her. She said I could do it only "over her dead body". She knew how content I was in Oxford. She was sure she would die before me and thought I would collapse if I did not have Oxford and my work to keep me going. She wanted me to continue doing what I always did, to be happy, to live, to go on. I am trying to.

Monique lived a decade longer than her mother and a few years longer than her father. We both knew that the age of one's parents is a good predictor of the longevity of their children. In any event, she must have felt that her days were numbered because for a few months before her death on 8 March she refused to discuss our plans for the summer of 2023. Going to her ancestral village, in the *département* of Gard, was one of the highlights of her year, and she had never missed spending a month or so there every summer. She always planned in advance the annual dates for Brignon.

She made it clear that she was to be buried in the little mausoleum with her parents and that I should one day be buried with her. I promised her I would. For a Jew to be buried in a Christian cemetery is quite a challenge, and I knew my sons would not be thrilled. But we talked about it and they understood.

In the summer of 2022, our stay in Brignon had to be shorter than usual because I had agreed to teach for two months at the NYU Law School. This forced us to leave Brignon before the end of August, when NYU Law School's semester begins. Monique was disappointed but, as always, was a good sport. I promised her that I would no longer accept commitments that clashed with her stays in Brignon.

As it happened, she fell and broke her pelvis before the end of my 2022 seminar and had to be hospitalized. I flew back before my last class to be with her in the hospital and afterwards when she was moved to a rehabilitation centre in Belleville in the 14th *arrondissement* of Paris, where she was so miserable. She had to lie constantly, as stepping on her feet could paralyse her legs. I visited her daily for seven weeks to cheer her up.

For early 2023, I planned to teach at NYU in March–April. Because of her declining eyesight, I raised with her the possibility of cancelling my NYU seminar. Monique insisted that I honour my commitment, especially because the students who had registered for it might lose an academic year and those who were in their final year would not be able to graduate. So on Tuesday, 26 February, I flew by Air France to JFK. When I called her from my Law School apartment in lower Manhattan later on Wednesday, she did not sound her usual self and said she was worried about her legs supporting her. I suggested that she go to bed and have a good rest. She said she would.

When I called on Thursday morning there was no answer. I thought that one of her friends could have taken her for a walk. After repeated attempts I got hold of Violaine de Villemeur, a neighbour, who fetched the caretaker, and together they opened the apartment. They found Monique in the bedroom, lying on the floor. She seems to have woken up when they came in, and could still speak. Despite our suggestions, she did not want to call a doctor or be taken to a hospital. But on Saturday morning, they found her much worse and she was moved to St Joseph's Hospital, which has a reputable neurological department. During the day I managed to call the hospital and spoke to a physician in intensive care. He said that Monique had had a stroke, that her right side was paralysed but her mind was lucid. Her life was not in danger, he told me. I flew to Paris on Saturday night, in anguish and blaming myself for what had happened.

I arrived at Charles de Gaulle airport after a sleepless night. The doctor with whom I spoke from New York had left instructions to let me enter the intensive-care floor although it was before the normal visiting hours. Kindly, he came to see me soon after my arrival. He still thought that her life was not in danger, but after seeing Monique I was not reassured. It was a bit of a shock to see her because her facial bone on the left side was sticking out a bit – she must have fallen on her face when she fainted – and the face itself appeared a little crooked. Her eyes were open, but I did not have the impression she could see me. I spoke to her. Obviously, she recognized my voice and stretched out her left hand and clutched my right hand. She could not speak and tried to whisper. I thought I understood her saying "I love you". These were the last words I heard from her. As I sat next to her, time stood still – or perhaps it passed too fast. And memories flashed back, especially of our meeting and falling in love.

It was the summer of 1980. I was invited to give a short, one-week course in the Hague Academy of International Law on the international civil service. As Monique was a UN civil servant and a translator specializing in legal matters, she decided to attend and enrolled in the programme. In the intervals between lectures, we started talking to each other. Back in New York I thought about her a lot. When she came to New York to start work as a translator at the United Nations, we quickly fell in love.

I was fifty at the time, and Monique was forty-six. I did not think that people of that age could fall in love so suddenly, so deeply, so desperately. What touched me tremendously was that when we met in Washington Square Park or Central Park on her visits to New York for the UN, she would run, not walk, towards me when she spotted me.

She later told me that what made her interested in me at first was my Holocaust experience. Her extended family in Marseille had saved a number of Jews at great risk to themselves. Her uncle Etienne Surjous, who was in charge of Tunisian affairs in the prefecture of Marseille, gave Jews exit permits to Tunisia. He was arrested by the SS and sentenced to death but liberated in time by the American forces, which had just landed in the South of France. He was made an Officer of the Legion of Honour. I keep his medal together with mine. And I have the original of his SS arrest warrant on the wall of Meron Room in Trinity College. It was delivered to his wife Mariette by an SS corporal. It's amazing how murderers could be so perversely legalistic.

What endeared Monique to me from the very beginning was our shared love of old castles, especially ruins, and of the sea, rivers and forests. And, of course, music. I had always loved classical music, but she made me a great devotee of Bach (especially of the Passions), Mozart, Purcell and Schubert. The first performances to which we went together in New York were of the *Winterreise* and *Messiah*.

Monique combined gentleness and tact with a character of steel when it came to questions of principle and integrity. Without her I would not have been able to survive many challenges in my life, including the Gotovina acquittal affair. Nor could I have coped with some other challenges. Now that she is gone, I have lost my compass.

∞

One of the most painful aspects of those terrible days in St Joseph's Hospital is that I came too late to have a last conversation, a single exchange with the person who was the great love of my life. In the remaining three or four days of her life, I was sitting on her left side, holding her hand, kissing her, talking to her about everything and nothing, praying to God to heal her miraculously or just keep her alive: "Oh God, do not take her away from me!" I don't think I ever prayed so much in my life, even when escaping Nazi executioners.

Despite my prayers, things went from bad to worse. On Monday, the paralysis spread to the right part of the body. I could only hold an inert limb, but she was still with me. On Tuesday, she stopped reacting. Her mind must have been destroyed and she went into a coma. The last two nights I was allowed to spend with her. The staff gave me a mattress to stay by her side. I preferred to sit on a chair so as to be closer to her, talk to her, hold her listless hand.

On Wednesday morning, a nurse suggested I go home to take a shower. I caught the metro, as it was likely to be faster than a taxi. On the way, my telephone rang. The duty nurse told me Monique had died at 10 o'clock, shortly after I left. Could I come back at once? When I arrived, the nurse told me that it is quite common that at the end of one's life, people delay dying until they can no longer hear the voice of their loved one. And so the joy of my life was gone. It was Wednesday, 8 March, just five days before the forty-second anniversary of our marriage.

The nurse said that I had a few hours to sit with Monique, undisturbed. And I did. I held her, talked to her, took photos of her, until the nurses came to tell me that it was warm in the room and it would be better to take the body to the hospital morgue. I agreed.

Thanks to the efficient help of Pierre Cauzid, a distant relative of Monique and a friend in Brignon, we managed to hold the burial on Saturday morning. She was buried in the little Protestant cemetery, a touchingly small, green, calm place with plenty of trees and a view of the hills nearby. A little group of friends and relatives came. I asked Maya, a friend of Monique, to speak. She said that Monique became a happy person only after we met.

As I could not cope with the emptiness left by Monique in her Brignon house, I took the train back to Paris later that same day. The apartment in Paris also felt terribly lonely. I was meant to co-lead an ICRC seminar for diplomats at NYU on Wednesday and Thursday. I knew Monique would want me to go. She had always admired the ICRC and would never agree to my not keeping a commitment, particularly to the ICRC, because of her. So I flew to New York on Monday. I was afraid I would break down when I spoke to the group. Miraculously, my voice held strong and I managed to sound cool and professional.

The ICRC had a surprise for me. As this was the fortieth anniversary of this annual seminar, they held a half-hour tribute for me, and prepared a pamphlet with quotes from selected participants over the years. Monique would have been happy and proud to listen to the tributes.

My prayers still may have served a purpose: not in God's healing Monique, but in allowing her to die quickly, painlessly and with dignity. She would not have wanted to live paralysed in body and mind. In the beginning my pain was too sharp to think so. But now, after a while, I thank God for taking her in peace. I thank Him also for bringing Monique into my life. I know my life has been extraordinary and not without miracles, but most of all I will always treasure the miracle of Monique.

APPENDIX

Milestones in my academic career

In 1984–5 I spent the whole academic year at the Max Planck Institute on Public International Law in Heidelberg. The book I wrote there, *Human Rights Law-Making in the United Nations*, received the annual best book prize of the American Society of International Law.

In 1989 and again in 1991, I was elected a visiting fellow of All Souls College, Oxford.

In 1992 I was elected to the Council on Foreign Relations.

In 1997 I was elected to membership of the very prestigious Institute of International Law, which is based in Strasbourg.

In 1999–2000, I spent the first semester at Harvard Law School and the second in Berkeley. I had never dreamt that I would return to Harvard to teach.

In 2003 I gave a general course at the Hague Academy of International Law.

In 2004 I received the Rule of Law Award of the International Bar Association.

APPENDIX

In 2006, I was named Charles L. Denison Professor in the NYU School of Law and the recipient of the Manley O. Hudson Medal of the American Society of International Law, given "in recognition of exceptional contributions to scholarship and international law".

In 2008, I received the Charles Homer Haskins Prize of the American Council of Learned Societies, the first lawyer to receive this prize, which is usually awarded to scholars in the humanities.

In 2009, I was elected a fellow of the American Academy of Arts and Sciences, no doubt thanks to my Shakespeare writings.

In 2010, I was elected honorary president of the American Society of International Law.

In 2011, I received a doctorate *honoris causa* from the University of Warsaw.

In 2014–15, I was appointed a visiting professor of law in Oxford, an appointment since renewed every three years.

In 2016, I was elected a visiting fellow of Mansfield College, Oxford, an appointment which is still continuing.

In 2021, I was elected an honorary fellow of Trinity College, Oxford (I was already a visiting honorary fellow), an appointment for life.

In 2021, I received an honorary doctorate from the University of Calisia, and was made an honorary citizen of Kalisz, the city where I was born.

APPENDIX

POEMS FOR MONIQUE

You Touched Me So

You touched me so
I did not know
Was my pain
All in vain
No, it was true
Because of you

A Complaint

Why do you choose the best
Your afflictions to test
Did you aim at her eyes
As her first sacrifice
To make her see all black
And be a living wreck
Could you not heal her sore
Or wait a little more
In your tenacity
Pitiless alacrity
You took her without agony
Leaving me solitude, grief and misery

In the Old Village Cemetery

Weeds and decaying leaves
Cypress and olive trees
Neglected, crumbling walls
A resting place for souls

APPENDIX

Graves all alone
Grief that my heart tore
Silence of a small village
A sleepy, lazy image,
Family mausoleum
I will not sing Te Deum
No one in sight
Spider webs all around
I used to come and pray
And thank your parents for the gift of you one blessed day
Now I pray for your serenity
Complaining to God for this fatality
Of taking you from me
Yesterday in the open pine coffin I kissed your cold lips
Now I kiss your sealed coffin
Before it's laid down there
In your family's grave
One day my coffin too
Will lie there with you
Our bones resting together
In our final embrace

Kyrie eleison

Just for an Instant

Do send her on a furlough
So she can fly below
Just for an instant
All this distance
Be it in a dream
Transported by a beam
Let her come as she was

APPENDIX

Without her angels' host
And without her halo
Just with her own glow
Telling me she loves me so
And she can see me still
And feel my body's chill
She whispers, do not cry
And kisses me goodbye